Echoes of War

Also by Robert Westall

NOVELS

The Machine-Gunners
The Wind Eye
The Watch-House
The Devil on the Road
Fathom Five
The Scarecrows
Futuretrack 5
The Cats of Seroster
Urn Burial
The Creature in the Dark
Ghost Abbey
Blitzcat
Old Man on a Horse
The Promise
If Cats Could Fly . . .
Stormsearch
The Kingdom by the Sea

STORIES

Break of Dark
The Haunting of Chas McGill
Rachel and the Angel
Ghosts and Journeys
A Walk on the Wild Side
The Call

ECHOES
of WAR

Robert Westall

Farrar, Straus and Giroux
New York

For Steve of Britannia Airlines,
who gave me the technical gen

Contents

Adolf

I first met Adolf when I was going to the off-licence for my dad's lager. He was standing at his front door, half-way down Tennyson Terrace. I remember walking down that dark, little side-street, and there was this one front door open, and a band of light lying across the pavement. Something made me think it was a bit odd, so I crossed the street to get as far away as possible. But as I crept past, a harsh voice called out,

'Boy!'

I didn't like the voice, or the bossy way it called. But I'm nosy (it gets me into trouble, sometimes), so I turned back and went across.

I couldn't see much of him, 'cos his back was against the light. But he stood very upright, and from his voice and the smell of him close-to, I could tell he was old and a foreigner.

'What's your name, boy?'

'Billy Martin,' I said grudgingly. I didn't want to tell him even that much.

'Billy Martin? *Gut!*'

He seemed to come to some decision and said, 'Will you go to the shop for me, Billy Martin? The offie?'

1

I didn't want to be bothered, but somehow I felt it would make more bother to say 'no'.

'Yeah. Why not?'

'*Gut*. Here is my list. And here is money. Be quick, please – I have not eaten yet.'

It made me feel like I was his *servant*. I'd have liked to have said 'no' then, all right. But I'd said yes, hadn't I? So when he put two bits of paper in my hand, I just took them. It wasn't until I'd walked to the next street-lamp that I saw one of the bits of paper was a fifty-pound note. That shook me, I can tell you. I mean, the temptation to run off with it was pretty strong. People shouldn't be allowed to tempt kids like that! I mean, giving a fifty-pound note to a total stranger!

But I'm not the sort to look for trouble. Not on a Thursday night, when I'm looking forward to a can of lager, and Anneka Rice's bum in *Treasure Hunt*. So I was determined to see he got his change down to the last penny. I was that angry with him, see?

When I got into the offie, I found it was easier said than done. His list was all in funny spiky writing. He wanted seven eggs, for some reason best known to himself, and there was that funny bar across the figure seven. I was still scratching my head when Jack Simms, who runs the offie, said,

'Old Adolf got you running errands for him? Give it me, I can read his writing.'

That's how I found out his name was Adolf.

I got Jack Simms to write down the price of everything and total it up, and I counted Adolf's change carefully before I left the shop. Put it in my right-hand pocket, and Dad's change in my left.

2

'Don't want no trouble,' I explained to Simms.

'He's a funny old bugger,' said Simms, agreeing.

When I knocked at Adolf's front door, I heard him call out, 'Come. It is not locked.'

I didn't like that. I'd rather have handed over the stuff in the street. Felt a bit like a fly walking into a spider's web. But I'm big for my age, and he was an old man. I told myself not to be daft.

His front room was big and brightly lit and stunk like a paint factory. Adolf was sitting in an old wooden rocker, with a big black cat on his lap. I put the carrier full of groceries on the wooden table beside him, and put the change in his hand and waited. He checked the groceries carefully, then checked the list and counted his change. Then he said '*Gut*' and looked up at me. He had very pale blue eyes, bulgy. They seemed to look straight through me.

I dropped my eyes first. But I remember I noticed his long nose and little white moustache, and the white hair combed hard across from the right. He was very wrinkly.

Then he said, '*Gut*. You are an honest child.'

'I'm not a child. I'm fourteen.'

'Children always wish to be grown up before their time. It was the same in the Hitler *jugend*.'

I didn't understand the word then. But it made me uneasy, the ugly, foreign sound of it. So I said,

'Gotta be going. Watching *Treasure Hunt* with me dad.'

'Do you not wish a reward for your work?'

The sarky way he asked made me mad. 'We British don't take money for running errands. Had to go to the offie for me dad anyway.'

'How righteous! The British are always righteous. It is

always the *foreign* football fans who start the fights.' You could tell he hated us British like poison, so I just turned on my heel to walk out.

And then I saw the painting he had done. It stood on an easel next to the door. You could tell from the smell that it was still wet. Great thick dabs of paint. Should've been a right mess, but it wasn't. It was a view of our town square, from high up, with the parish church. Really good. The crowds of little people were only rough dabs of paint, but they seemed to be walking, when you looked at them.

'That's smart,' I said. 'The people are really walking.' It just burst out of me.

He made a noise behind me like a snort of disgust. But you could tell he was a bit pleased, really.

Then he said,

'I need shopping on Tuesdays and Thursdays and Saturdays. Will you go for me? I will pay you fifty pence for each trip.'

I stared at him.

'I myself cannot do it. I have a stiff leg.' He wasn't asking for sympathy. Just telling me. You could tell he hated having a stiff leg. So I said OK. It wasn't any bother. I go most nights for Dad anyway.

And his paintings interested me. I could see other ones now, stacked against the walls. All local scenes, buildings and people. All good, but they made Cromborough look as if the sun never shone – as if there was always a big dark thunderstorm hanging over the town. As if something terrible was going to happen, like the end of the world or something.

'Do you sell them?' I asked.

He smiled a sour smile. 'When I was young, I wished

4

only to be an artist. But my father wished me to be civil servant. My father thought being civil servant was the greatest thing in the world. And then came my fight – my fight against evil. Now I am old, yes, I paint to stay alive.'

His eyes no longer looked straight through me. They were dreamy, far away, as if he was looking at Mount Everest or something. Gave me the creeps. So I said, to bring him back to earth,

'You shouldn't give total strangers fifty-pound notes. They mightn't come back with the change.'

He smiled; a really sneaky smile. 'I have watched you, boy. You come down this street every night at quarter to eight, and you return at eight. I know from the name on your carrier bag that you have been to the offie. If you had not come back, how long would it have taken the *polizei* to find Billy Martin? I am not a fool, and now I have proved that you are not a fool. I have no wish to be served by fools . . .' He held out a fifty-pence piece. 'Here is your first night's wages. Do not tell me there is any boy who cannot use fifty pence?'

I took it. It was warm from his old wrinkled hand. I didn't really want to take it. Felt I was selling my soul, somehow. But I took it and ran, though I was glad when it was spent and gone.

I was late for *Treasure Hunt*. And my dad was dying for his first mouthful of lager.

The next night I called, I'd made up my mind not to go in. But when I got back with his shopping, he said slyly,

'I have made a new painting, for myself alone. Do you not wish to see it? Many in this town would like to see it . . .'

5

It was enough to get me in.

He pulled a drape off the picture on the easel. It was in his usual style, and yet different. It was of our local Job Centre. Now, by sheer fluke, our Job Centre is much too posh for the job it does. Used to be the Railway Hotel, when we still had a railway. All marble columns and a gilded dome on top, but the gilt's half worn off now. But it still looks far too grand, and Adolf had made it look grander. And very posh and cosy inside, what you could see through the windows.

It's unfortunate that the Social Security people park their cars in front, because they're pretty posh cars, D and E reg, which can't cheer up the poor old dolies as they queue up for their Giro.

And Adolf had made the cars bigger and posher than they really were . . .

He'd painted the little figures of the dolies, going in looking totally fed up and coming out looking even more fed up, like they already knew where their money was going, and were still up to their eyebrows in debt. It was really very clever; he'd told the truth, but made it look so much *worse*.

'I didn't know you cared about the dolies,' I said. Because I couldn't think what else to say.

'I know them. Because I have been one. Long before the war. I left home, because I could not bear to become civil servant. I went to Vienna to become artist. But I became day-labourer instead, to stay alive. I stood in line every day, while the rich men in their fur collars inspected us like cattle. If they liked the look of us they hired us, and we knew we would eat that day. But the money was gone before night. Why should the poor think of tomorrow?

What does tomorrow offer the poor? When they have money, they eat and drink till it is gone. That is when I dreamed of my fight. To give the poor a steady wage, to make them prudent. To give them good food and strong bodies. To make their lives joyful, not endless drudgery.'

He had that dreamy look on his face again. It still gave me the creeps. So I said,

'Britain's not like that. Britain's not as bad as that . . .'

He looked at me with those pale, bulging, blue eyes. 'You are patriotic, because your father has money. But why should the poor be patriotic and wish to serve their country? What has their country ever done for them?'

I didn't like it. Didn't seem right. He was sort of turning the world upside down. And worse, he was starting to make me see things the same way. I didn't want any part in his fight. My dad makes a decent living going round repairing tellies; my mum works in our school canteen. We run a good car, and go to Marbella or Gran Canaria for a fortnight every year. And I'm going to get my GCSEs and work for Austin Rover as a tech. apprentice . . .

But if this old bugger started talking to the dolies . . . I was suddenly glad he had a stiff leg and couldn't get out of the house much.

'Gotta go now,' I said suddenly. 'My dad'll want his beer.'

'Ah, beer,' he said, still dreamy. 'I remember the *bier-kellers* – men would meet and sit and talk out their grievances, and plan to put the world right. Now they drink their beer at home, and watch the *verdammt* television.'

I just went.

Looking back, after his terrible end, I often wondered what

I thought he was, in the beginning. Just a funny old foreigner I suppose, who could paint pictures good enough to sell. He was certainly well off for a pensioner. His terrace-house was newly painted, and the high privet behind his railings neatly cut. His was the only house to have kept its front gate. And he kept himself very neat: grey trousers and a grey cardie and grey slippers. And he didn't smell – only of paint.

Why didn't I mention him to Dad? Because Dad's more the practical sort; a good bloke to have around if the car breaks down, or if you want new fence-posts putting in that won't fall down in a couple of years. But he's not a great bloke for talk. He always switches off discussion programmes on the telly – calls them 'talking-shops'. And he calls MPs of all parties 'big-mouths' and never votes at elections. And my mum is just interested in the garden and bus-trips with mobs of other women in her spare time. I sometimes wondered what would happen to the world if no one was more interested in running it than my mum and dad.

Certainly Adolf was keen on world events. He had this telly with teletext in the corner of his studio, and every so often he would click on the news headlines and look at something that President Bush or President Gorbachev had done and mutter 'Foolish, foolish' to himself. Once he said to me about Afghanistan,

'The Russians have no sense of history. You British failed in Afghanistan; the Russians should have learnt your lesson. They have thrown away a division of good soldiers. Any nation like Afghanistan, that lives only to fight, *cannot* be beaten.'

Other times he would be more cheerful. Offer me strange

dark coffee that he said was 'Genuine Viennese coffee – you will not get better in Vienna today.' It wasn't bad – I got to quite like it.

Sometimes he would get me to talk to his pets. He had two cats. One was a great fat tabby that he called Hermann. The other was the sneaky black one that would sidle up to you, friendly-like, then suddenly bite you. He called that one Heinrich. And he had a red-and-blue parrot, on a stand in the corner, that looked as old as the hills, like any other parrot. He said he called that Josef (with an 'f' he insisted) because when it spoke, it told nothing but lies. It talked a foreign language I couldn't understand. But no wonder. I gave up even French in the third year – I'm on the technical side, like Dad.

He talked to them all, like they were human. I expect he was lonely. I think, apart from me, he had no one else who he could really talk to. Though there was a cleaning woman who I never saw, who he called Little Eva.

I would ask about his pictures. He would chat away about the people in them. How when busy people met, they would talk half-way down a street, but idle people always stood around on street corners. How observant old ladies were, peering through their net curtains. 'They have lived their lives,' he would say. 'Now they can only live through the joys and sorrows of others.' There was usually an old lady peering out somewhere in his pictures, if you knew where to look for her.

There was only one picture he would never talk about. An odd picture of an old-fashioned railway-carriage, parked in the middle of a forest. He said only one thing about it ever, and he was pale and shaking with rage at the time. He said that railway-carriage was the most evil place in the world. The sorrows of all mankind were born in that railway-carriage.

He looked quite insane for a moment, then he changed the subject.

One night, though, he grabbed me in before I had even done his shopping.

'You must see my new picture that I have painted. I have caught the *truth*.' His hands were quivering as he grabbed my shoulders.

God, it was a *horrible* picture. Of some Middle Eastern country, because the buidings had flat roofs and were painted in pale colours.

What was left of them. Because they'd been blown to buggery. And underneath the fallen walls, little kids in what had been white nightshirts were lying dead. Just a head sticking out here, and a hand sticking out there. It was all the more horrible because it was highly detailed, not his usual slabby style. There seemed to be a crumpled newspaper photograph pinned to the corner of his easel, as if he'd been painting from it, but it was so covered with oil-painty fingerprints that you couldn't see what it was of any more.

'Who are they?' I asked, feeling quite sick.

'Palestinian children. The Jews did that. The Jews have learnt their lessons well. *They* invade without warning, now. *They* shoot unarmed protesters. *They* torture their prisoners, to make them confess. They conquer, they oppress. They have become the Chosen of God, the Master Race.'

Funny thing was, I couldn't tell whether he was con-demning them or approving of them. He just seemed crazy with excitement. 'That is the *truth*,' he kept on yelling. 'I have caught the *truth*.'

'But it's not all like that,' I shouted. 'The whole world's not like that. Not my mum and dad. Not *Britain*.'

'Oh, no,' he said. 'The British are not like that. The British do their evil far away, where they do not have to look at it. Like Dresden.'

'What you mean, Dresden?'

He grabbed my shoulders again. Hard. 'Do they not teach you about Dresden at school? How strange! Then I will teach you.' He forced me to sit down.

'Dresden was the prettiest town in Germany. A historic town, all made of old timber. No factories, except the one where the beautiful Dresden china was made. And in 1945, Dresden was full of women and children, fleeing from the Russians. A hundred thousand of them.

'And your fine RAF sent a thousand bombers and blew Dresden to pieces. Then they dropped incendiaries to set the wreckage on fire, so that those who were buried alive were roasted alive. All to please Stalin, when the war was already lost and won. That was Dresden, which they do not teach you at school.'

'Let me go,' I shouted and then ran out of the house, wiping the spit of his rage off my face as I went.

I never went back. As far as I was concerned he was a nutter, a dangerous old nutter.

But I couldn't get what he'd said about Dresden out of my mind. So finally I went and asked my history teacher. He didn't say much, just that there was a book about Bomber Command in the school library. I got it out at lunchtime and read it.

It admitted that Dresden had been bombed in 1945. It said it was a strategic rail-centre, and that the bombing had been in support of the advancing Red Army. And that was all.

I closed the book and thought thanks for nothing. That night I dreamt that I was in Dresden, roasting alive. I woke up rigid, in a cold sweat, and couldn't get back to sleep again. But somehow I knew that old Adolf had been right, and the British book was telling lies.

Jesus, you ever had that feeling? If you find one book telling lies, you wonder if all the other books aren't telling lies as well. There I was, reading all those books for GCSE, like a good little boy, and they might *all* be lies. I had to ask somebody, but *who*? Mum and Dad hadn't even been born when Dresden was bombed.

In the end I went back to my history teacher. Told him about the two versions of Dresden. He looked annoyed, yet shifty at the same time.

'You must use your own judgement, Martin. That's what we're here for. To teach you to use your own judgement, using primary sources and documents.'

'Like *what*? How do I find out how the Germans felt about the war?'

'Look, old lad. You mustn't get carried away. We're not even *doing* the Second World War for GCSE. You've got exams to pass this summer. Concentrate on those. You've got your career to think of . . .'

Christ, I hate it when they go on like that. I mean, they encourage you to think for yourself, then when you do, they get upset. So I went on yelling, 'Where's the book the Germans wrote?'

Maybe he just wanted to get rid of me. I don't think he

reckoned I'd ever find the book (and no wonder). So he just said, with a nasty, half-hidden grin,

'Hitler wrote a book called *Mein Kampf*. That was what started the Second World War.'

I looked for it in the school library. It wasn't there, of course. I asked the librarian, and she gave me a funny look and said, 'I hope you're not thinking of joining the National Front, Billy Martin.'

That should have warned me that I was living in the Red Republic of Cromborough, run by the Loony Left. But I just went down to the public library, and they hadn't got it on the shelves either. Fortunately they've taught us to use the microfiche system at school, so I sat down at the microfiche and went through all the non-fiction slides till I found 'Authors H A–G E'.

No 'Hitler, Adolf'. No *Mein Kampf*. Not a single copy in the whole Red Republic of Cromborough.

So I filled in a request card. *Mein Kampf* by Hitler, Adolf. I didn't know the publisher or the date, but it was hardly *Little Noddy Rides Again*. I gave the card to the woman on the inquiries counter with the last fifty-pence piece I'd had off old Adolf. The woman read the card and nearly went mad.

'Oh, you cheeky little idiot,' she shouts. 'Is this your idea of a joke? Wasting my time and the library's request cards?'

'I really want it,' I said. 'Honest!'

Up comes the Chief Librarian, a fat bloke with spectacles.

'What seems to be the trouble, Mrs Seddon?'

She gave him the card, tight-lipped. He read it, tight-lipped, then tore it up and gave me my fifty pence back, with a slam into my hand, as if he would have liked to clonk me one. Then he said,

'Go away, or I'll call the police.'

I knew there was no point in arguing. When they get that look on their faces . . .

But as I told you before, I'm nosy. And the more people don't want me to know something, the more I want to know it. And I knew where to go. The dirty second-hand bookshop in Wythenshawe Street. A huge old place, full of shifty-looking blokes fumbling the stuff on the shelves. I've been chucked out dozens of times, once the owner's finished serving somebody else. He always asks me what book I want, very sharp, and then says he hasn't got it, quick, without even looking on the shelves.

Anyway, this happened as usual. But when I said *Mein Kampf* he went a bit thoughtful, and his eyes got that greedy glint. He'll sell anybody anything for money.

'Gotta copy. But it's seventeen pounds to you.'

That was a facer, because I only had twenty-one pounds in the Post Office, saved up for our next trip to Gran Canaria.

'Can I sell it back to you afterwards?' I asked.

'Give you ten pounds for it. If it's still in mint condition.' Greedy sod.

'Let's see it,' I said, in case he was pulling a fast one, and selling me something written in German.

But it was in English, translated in 1937. With a fore-word very respectful towards Hitler. And lots of pictures of Hitler striding around wet streets in a belted raincoat, looking like he's worried and going to give someone a piece of his mind. A big fat book, like an encyclopaedia . . .

So I gave the bloke fifty pence deposit, and he said he'd put it by till the end of the week. But I drew out the money next evening, and picked up the book on the way home. My mother noticed me carrying it and asked what it was, but I'd got a bit wary by that time and said it was just a schoolbook for homework.

Well, once in my bedroom, it was a revelation. I suppose it would've been boring to any other kid, 'cos Hitler certainly didn't have a style like James Bond. But it was all there.

All the things *my* Adolf had said. About wanting to be an artist, and his rows with his father, who wanted him to be a civil servant. (He was terribly respectful about his father, even though they had had all those rows which made him leave home.) And about being a day-labourer, and the plight of the poor, and his fight against evil, which in German was *mein kampf* – my fight.

What a facer! And then I began looking at the pictures of Hitler: those bulging eyes that looked straight through you; that little moustache; that hair brushed across hard from the right. Just like *my* Adolf. And when my Adolf had criticized Bush or Gorbachev, he'd spoken about them like he was their equal, like he understood what their problems were . . .

God, I knew about the Nazi war-criminals hiding in Brazil and Paraguay, and the trial of Eichmann and that John Demjanyuk. And people saying there were war-criminals still hiding out in Britain.

But could Hitler really have escaped from the Berlin bunker and be living half-way down Tennyson Terrace?

I didn't get much sleep that night, I can tell you.

I kept it to myself for a week. Who could I tell? I thought of telling Dad. But he was watching *Tomorrow's World*. I thought of telling Mum, but she was busy getting the tea. I thought of telling my history teacher, but I knew he'd just take the piss out of me, and I'd be the laughing-stock of the staff room.

Which is why, in the end, I told Gaz Higgins. Which was my big mistake. Gaz is the brightest kid in our class. He's got an open mind. Trouble is, he's also got an open mouth. If you want everyone in the school to know something, tell Gaz Higgins it's your most precious secret.

Anyway, he didn't laugh at me. He got quite excited, especially when I mentioned my Adolf's paintings. He's quite keen on art, 'cos he wants to be a famous cartoonist with the *Sun* when he grows up, and get to chat up the Page Three birds. He said he had an old colour supplement at home, full of Hitler's paintings.

He brought it to school next day. God, they were the same kind of paintings. Pictures of grand big buildings in Vienna done with the same broad brushstrokes, and with the same dark sky all thunderclouds, and a feeling that something terrible was going to happen. Only the young Hitler hadn't been so keen on painting little people scurrying around – there were hardly any people in *his* pictures at all.

'It's him,' I said. 'He still paints the same.'

'I'm not surprised he came to England,' said Gaz. 'He lived in Liverpool a bit before the war. His cousin kept a boarding-house there – his name was Alois Hitler. I saw a play about it on the telly.'

The bell went for afternoon school then, and we didn't say much more because he had double-art and I had double-history. He didn't say much more to me about it ever, really.

But he must have said plenty to other people. Considering what happened afterwards.

I first noticed it, going down to the offie one night. I always slunk past on the other side of the street now, frightened Adolf would spot me. Though it wasn't a Tuesday or a Thursday or a Saturday night . . .

But even from the other side of the street, by the dim light of the next street-lamp, I could see people had been daubing on Adolf's garden wall. A couple of small swastikas.

Next night the swastikas were bigger. And by the end of the week, NF symbols were appearing.

By the next Monday night, someone had aerosolled WAR CRIMINAL and KILL THE JEWS and a star of David in yellow.

By the end of that week, I began to notice groups of kids hanging round in twos and threes. Not local kids. Punks with four-packs of beer, shouting weird things at the house and kicking each other with their big boots. As if they were waiting for something to happen. More every night I passed.

There was never any sign of Adolf, but that didn't seem to discourage them. I began getting very worried, because whatever Adolf had once done, he was now a lame old man, and those punks and skinheads aren't funny, once they get their eye on you.

But I didn't know what to do. There was still nobody I could talk to about it.

Then, on the Wednesday night, my dad was sitting reading through the news in the local paper, on his way to the car ads. And he stops and says,

'That big-mouth Harrington's really done it this time.'

'What's he done, Dad?'

Harrington was a far-Left Labour councillor and Dad's real pet hate. Every week Harrington finds some reason to get his name in the paper. Everything, to Harrington, is 'a public scandal' or 'a creeping threat to the underprivileged of Cromborough.' If he gets really stuck, he'll make a round of the public lavatories and make a fuss about *them*.

'He's gone too far . . . he's gone off his chump properly. He reckons there's a top Nazi war-criminal living in Tennyson Terrace, and he can't even spell incognito properly. Two ts. Pig ignorant, that man. I hope the bloke does him for libel . . .'

My heart sank into my boots. 'What's the war-criminal's name, Dad?' I quavered.

'Doesn't give it. Even he's not *that* big a fool.'

'Dad,' I said, taking a deep breath. 'I know the bloke he means. I think it's Adolf Hitler hisself.'

'Yewhat?' shouts Dad, for once paying full attention to something other than motor cars.

So I told him everything.

'Jesus Christ, our Billy,' says Dad, 'ye're more barmy than old Harrington. Where have you got all this rubbish from? Hitler was old when he died in 1945. If he was alive now he'd be a hundred and five or something. How old's this bloke down Tennyson Terrace?'

'Dunno,' I said. 'Pretty old. All old people look alike.' But I knew I'd been a total idiot. My Adolf was nowhere near that age. 'About as old as Grandpa, I think.'

'Christ, Billy, your Grandpa's only *sixty-eight*.'

Then I told Dad about the daubing on Adolf's wall, and the skinheads and punks who were hanging about.

'This is serious,' said Dad. 'We're going to have to get this sorted, afore something worse happens. Where's me coat?'

'Aw, Dad, leave it. It'll blow over.' I was scared of facing Adolf again, after what I'd done. 'He's a nasty old sod. He can look after himself. He's as sharp as a wagonload of monkeys.'

'You're coming wi' me,' says Dad, grabbing me. 'I've got no money to pay for a case of libel. You're going to go down there an' apologize. Then we'll put things right wi' the newspaper.'

Just then Mum comes in from her Townswomen's Guild choir practice. 'There's trouble brewing down Tennyson Terrace,' she says. 'A whole mob of skinheads. I was scared to walk past the end of the street . . .'

'C'mon,' shouts Dad as he whizzes out the front door. I was never so proud of him in my life. Or so ashamed of myself.

As we turned the corner of Tennyson Terrace (and me mam came too, though she didn't look like she wanted to), we heard the skinheads shouting 'A-DOLF A-DOLF A-DOLF' in that awful rhythmic way they have. And then, beyond the huddled crowd, there was a sudden flare of yellow light, and the crash of glass.

'They're throwing petrol,' shouts Dad. 'Go home, Renee. Go home quick an' ring the police.' And my mum doesn't argue.

There's three more flares and crashes before we reach the back of the crowd. I think they must have thrown one through the studio window, because it was all alight inside. It must have caught easily, with all that oil-paint. The front door was alight as well, with burning petrol dribbling down the doorstep. Only the upstairs was still dark.

My dad tore through the skinheads, shoving them left and right. I was scared they'd beat him to a pulp, but all their eyes were feasting themselves on the burning house. I don't think they even noticed Dad, no more than if he was a fly, no matter how much he cursed and pushed them.

And there wasn't another grown-up in sight: not even a face in any of the neighbouring windows. Cowering bastards!

But it meant Dad and I were right at the front when old Adolf pushed open his upstairs bedroom window. Smoke trickled out past him and you could see a bit of flame-light already flickering behind in the bedroom doorway.

He only shouted one thing. I'll never forget it. He shouted,

'Even if I was Hitler, am I any worse than you?'

Then the smoke got to his lungs, and he doubled up coughing, and we never saw him again.

Then we heard the police sirens coming from three different directions at once. And all those skinheads took to their brave British heels.

It was all in the local paper the following week.

HOUSE OF WAR-HERO PETROL-BOMBED.

Police are seeking the gang of skinheads who petrol-bombed, last Wednesday night, the home of Warrant-Officer Adolf Krainer, late of the Polish Air Force. Warrant-Officer Krainer, who is recovering in a Leeds hospital, had lived in Cromborough since being invalided out of the air force in 1945 with a thigh wound sustained while bombing Germany. He flew sixty-seven missions and was awarded the Air Force Cross for nursing his Lancaster home on two engines after his last mission to Dresden.

In his early days in Cromborough, he was a founder member of the Polish Club and chairman of the Anglo-German Friendship Society, which arranged exchange-trips for schoolchildren between Cromborough and Dresden. He was well known as a painter and exhibited in London and Leeds.

In recent years, he increasingly lived the life of a recluse.

His home was gutted, in spite of the best efforts of Cromborough Fire Brigade.

When recovered, he will live with friends in Leeds.

'He was never quite right in the head,' said old Simms to my dad in the offie. Since the fire Dad's walked down with me to collect the lager, 'cos I'm nervous now. Not of skinheads, but of Adolf Krainer's burnt-out house, watching me.

'Never normal,' continued Simms, 'not since he first came to the town. Always going on about Dresden, and all those little German kids who were burnt alive. Made your flesh creep to hear him. That's why he started the Friendship Society, but it never cured his guilt.

'Always going on about the Treaty of Versailles in 1919 – reckoned the Germans got a bad deal in that railway-carriage at Fontainebleau. He said it sowed the seeds of the Second World War.

'He even saw good in Hitler. Many's the night I've heard him defend Hitler and that book *Mein Kampf* in this very shop – I thought sometimes some bloke would knock him flat for it.

'In fact,' went on Simms, lowering his voice, 'I reckon he read that *Mein Kampf* too often, when he was sitting alone. It sort of took him over. He even got to look a bit like Hitler in the end – the way he combed his hair, and that little tash. Did you ever meet him?'

'No,' said Dad hurriedly, with a worried look at me. 'No, I never did.'

'War does funny things to people – years after,' said Simms. 'Old Krainer started off fighting Hitler, and ended up thinking he *was* Hitler. I'm glad I was only on the anti-aircraft guns meself – outside Lowestoft . . .'

Dad and I picked up our lager and left.

The blank windows of the gutted house of Adolf Krainer seemed to follow us like eyes, the whole length of Tennyson Terrace.

Gifts from the Sea

The next bomb was the closest yet. Its slow, descending screech got louder and louder and louder.

Brian began to count under his breath. If you were still counting when you reached ten, you knew it hadn't blown you to pieces. He stared at the curving white wall of the shelter, the candle flickering in its saucer. The last things he might ever see on this earth . . .

Seven, eight, nine . . . the bunk he was lying on kicked like a horse. The candle fell over and rolled round the saucer, still burning, and starting to drip wax on to the little table. From the top bunk, his mother reached with a nearly steady hand and set it upright again. They listened to the sound of falling bricks as a house collapsed, the rain of wood and broken slates pattering down on the road and thudding on to the earth on top of their shelter.

'Some poor bugger's gotten it,' said Mam.

After the all-clear had gone, they climbed out wearily into the dawn and saw which poor bugger had gotten it. Number ten was just a pile of bricks. Eight and twelve had lost their windows and half the slates off their roofs. The road was littered. A big black dog was running around in circles, barking at everything and everybody. An ambulance was just disappearing round the corner of the road, and a crowd of people were breaking up, where number ten had been. Dad came across, filthy in his warden's uniform. Mam stared at his face silently, biting her lip.

'It's all right, hinny.' He grinned, teeth very white in his black face. 'They were in the shelter. We got them out. They're not hurt. But she cried when she saw what was left of her house.'

'She kept it like a little palace,' said Mam. 'She was that proud of it.'

Dad looked up at the sky, the way the German bombers had gone.

'Aye, well,' he said, 'the RAF lads got one of the buggers.'

They trailed round to the back door of their house. The kitchen seemed just as they'd left it; only a little jug with roses on it had fallen on the floor and broken into a hundred fragments.

'That was a wedding present,' said Mam. 'Your Auntie Florrie gave us that.' She bent down wearily and began picking up the pieces.

But it was when they opened the front-room door that they gasped. The windows were still whole, and the curtains intact. But everything else was just heaps of whiteness, as if there'd been a snowstorm.

'Ceiling's down,' said Dad. Brian stared up at where the ceiling had been. Just an interesting pattern of inch-wide laths, nailed to the joists. Dad ran upstairs and shouted that the bedroom ceilings were down too.

'Eeh, what a mess,' said Mam. 'How we ever going to get this straight?' Brian could tell she was on the verge of tears. 'Me best room. Where can I put the vicar now, if he calls . . .'

'Just thank God you've still got a house to clean, hinny,' said Dad gently. 'But,' he added, looking at Brian, *'you'd* better go and stay at your gran's, till we get this lot cleared up.'

An hour later, still unwashed, still without breakfast, Brian was on the little electric train down to the coast. He had Mam's real leather attaché-case on the seat beside him, with a change of underpants, pyjamas, a hot-water bottle and his five best Dinkie toys. He felt empty and peculiar, but excited. An adventure; you couldn't say he was running away like those evacuee kids. Gran, at the coast, was nearer the Jerry bombers than home. It was more like a holiday; no school for a week. And even more like a holiday because he was setting out before most kids were up. The train was full of men going to work in the shipyards. Blackened overalls and the jackets of old pinstripe suits; greasy caps pulled down over their eyes as they dozed. Everybody grabbed a nap when they could these days. But they all looked like his dad, so he felt quite safe with them.

He turned and looked out of the window, down at the river far below. Greasy old river, with brilliant swirls of oil on it. Packed with ships, docked three-deep on each bank. Big tankers; the rusty grey shapes of destroyers and corvettes. Already some welders were at work, sending down showers of brilliant electric-blue sparks, like fireworks in the dull grey morning.

Britain can make it, thought Brian. Britain can take it. He often heard Mr Churchill talking inside his head, especially when he felt tired or fed up. It helped.

The man beside him spoke to the man opposite. 'Aah see Gateshead's playin' Manchester City on Saturday.'

'Andy Dudgeon'll hold them.'

'City's good . . .'

'Andy'll still hold them.'

Brian was last to get out. At Tynemouth. He walked down empty Front Street, sniffing the smell of the sea that came to greet him. *Just* like being on holiday. A Co-op cart was delivering milk. Brian felt so good and grown up, he almost stopped and told the milkman all about being bombed. But only a kid would've done that, so he only said good-morning.

Gran gave him a good breakfast. She cut her toast much thicker than Mam, and always burnt the edges in an interesting way because she toasted it with a fork on the open fire. It tasted strongly of soot, but there was a huge lump of butter in the dish that made up for it. He didn't ask where the butter had come from; he'd just be told that Granda knew a feller who worked down the docks.

After breakfast he helped Granda hoist the Union Jack on the wireless-mast in front of the row of coastguard cottages on the cliff. An act of defiance against Hitler. Granda ran it up the pole, broke out the tightly wrapped bundle with a vigorous tug on the rope. The flag fluttered bravely in the wind. Granda said 'God save the King' and they both saluted the flag. Then Granda said 'God help the workers', but that was just a joke. They always did it the same, when he stayed with Granda. Then Granda went to work, and Gran got out the poss-tub and the poss-stick, it being Monday morning, and started thumping the washing in the water as if Fatty Goering was somewhere down there in a midget submarine.

Washing day was no time to be in the house. Wet washing

hung in front of the fire, steam billowed, the windows misted up and even your hands felt damp. Brian got out, followed by a yell that twelve o'clock was dinner-time.

Everything was still terribly *early*. Brian felt hopelessly ahead of himself. Still, he had plenty of *plans*. First he called at the school, to stand grandly outside the railings and watch the local kids being marched in, and feel *free* himself. Then he went on to tour the defences; the sandbagged anti-aircraft pom-poms on the sea-front. He spent a long time hovering from foot to foot, enjoying the guns' shining, oily evilness, till a grumpy sentry asked him why he wasn't in school.

Then he headed down the pier. The pier was like a road, running half a mile out into the grey of the sea. It was like walking on the water. It was like walking into the wide blue yonder, like the song of the American Army Air Corps. It was like playing dare with the Nazis, across the sea in Norway. It was even better when waves were breaking over the granite wall, as they were today. You tiptoed along, listening for the sound of the next wave, and if you were lucky you just managed to duck down behind the wall before the wave broke, and stayed dry. Otherwise you got soaked to the skin, all down your front.

He dodged successfully all the way, feeling more and more omnipotent. At the far end he stood in the shelter of the enormous lighthouse and watched an armed trawler put to sea. It came speeding up the smooth water of the estuary, and then pitched like a bucking bronco as it was hit by the first sea wave. The wind blew its sooty smell right up to him, with the smell of grilling kippers from the galley chimney. Soot, salt, wind, spray and kippers blew around his head, so that he shouted out loud for joy, and waved to the men on the deck; and one of them waved back.

And then he suddenly felt lonely, out there so close to Hitler. Getting back to land was harder and scarier. The waves might creep up behind your back; so might a German bomber. They'd machine-gunned the lighthouse before now; they would machine-gun anything that moved, and most things that didn't. He took much longer getting back to shore, running sideways like a crab, looking back over his shoulder for waves and Germans.

At the end of the pier he met a dog, on the loose like himself. A big Alsatian, all wet and spiky-haired from swimming in the river, and thirsting for mischief. It shook itself all over him, then put its paws on his shoulders and licked his face all over with a long, smooth, pinky-purple tongue.

Then it stood by the steps down to the rocks and barked encouragingly. Brian stood doubtful. It was good fun going round the tumbled rocks at the base of the Castle Cliff, but dicey. The cliff was brown and flaky and crumbling; there'd been falls of rock. When his dad was a boy it had been called Queen Victoria's Head because, seen sideways, it had looked just like the profile of the old Queen on a coin: nose, chin, bust, everything. Then the cliff had fallen and the Queen was gone, and now the cliff looked like nothing at all.

The boulders at the foot were huge and green with seaweed, with narrow cracks in between, where you could trap and break your ankle. And if you trapped your ankle or broke it, and you were alone except for a dog that didn't know you, you would just have to lie there till the tide came in and drowned you and swept your body out to sea.

Nobody else walked round Castle Cliff rocks on a week-day . . .

The dog barked, insisting. Brian looked at the line of damp on the rocks, and decided the tide was still going out.

He followed the dog out on to the rocks, waving his arms wildly as he leapt from boulder to boulder, and his hobnailed boots slithered on the green weed and only came to a crunching stop in the nick of time, as they met a patch of white barnacles.

But almost immediately he was glad he'd come. He began to find things brought in by the tide. First a glass fishing-float, caught in a veil of black, tarry net. He scrabbled aside the net; underneath, the float was thick, dark green glass, half the size of a football. He dropped it inside his shirt, where it lay cool and damp against his belt, because he had to have both hands free for the rocks. Mam would like the glass float for her mantelpiece; it would help make up for the damage the Nazis had done to her house.

Then there was a funny dark piece of wood, about as big as an owl. At some time it had had a bolt driven through it, for there was a dark round hole, like an eye, at one end. It had been burnt too. It had ridged feathers of damp, blue-black, shiny charcoal. Brian looked out to sea, remembering ships bombed and burnt and sunk by the Nazi bombers, within sight of the shore . . .

But the sea, and the grinding rocks, had worn the lump of wood into the shape of folded wings and a tail, so that when he held it out upright in his hand, it *did* look like a bird, with a round dark eye each side of its head. The dog thought it looked like a bird too. It ran up, barking frantically, and neatly snatched the bird from his hand with one slashing grab. Then it discovered it was only wet wood and let it drop. It barked at it some more, then looked at Brian, head on one side, baffled.

He picked it up and held it out at arm's length again, waggling it to make it look alive. And again the dog thought it was a bird, and leapt and grabbed. Then dropped it, shaking its head vigorously, to get the sharp taste of salt out of its mouth.

He threw it for the dog, as far towards the sea as he could. It hit a boulder and leapt in the air with a hollow clonk. On the rebound, the dog caught it and slithered wildly down a sloping rock, ending up with a splash in a deep rock-pool. It brought the piece of wood back to him, and shook itself all over him, soaking him anew.

The fourth time he threw it, it clonked down a crack in the rocks and vanished out of sight. The dog tried to get down after it, but couldn't, and stood barking instead. Brian was suddenly sad; he would have liked to have taken it home and given it to his dad. His dad might have set it on a base and varnished it and put it on the mantelpiece. His dad liked things like that. As he stood, he heard the cautious voice of his dad inside his head telling him to be careful, or he'd be a long time dead. It made him check on the state of the tide, but he was sure it was still going out.

But he explored more cautiously after that. Found evil-smelling cod's heads from the fish-gutting, hollow-eyed like skulls, with teeth sharp and brown as a mummified alligator. He sniffed at the stink of rotting flesh, was nearly sick, and sniffed more gently a second time, till finally he could stand the smell without being sick. It was part of toughening yourself up for the War Effort . . .

And then he found the patch of limpets, clinging to a

rock. He hovered again. Limpets were his great temptation. They clung to the rocks so hard, you might have thought them stuck there for ever with glue. But he'd found out long ago they weren't. Under the shallow cone of the ribbed shell was a sort of snail, which clung to the rock with a great big sucker-foot. If the limpet heard or felt you coming, it put on maximum suction and you'd never get it off the rock. But if you crept up quietly, you could get the blade of your knife under it before it knew you were there, and you could flick it off upside down into the palm of your hand.

And there it was, all pale soft folds, gently writhing in its bed of liquid, all beautiful with its two eyes coming out on stalks, like snails' eyes . . . It somehow gave him a squishy feeling, like the photos of semi-nude girls at the Windmill Theatre in London, which he snitched out of *Picture Post* after his parents had read it, and which he hid in an old tobacco-tin of his father's, under a pile of his own *War Illustrateds*.

He took his fill, till the feeling wore off, and then he carefully chose a smooth wet patch of rock and put the limpet back on it, right way up. He tested it; the limpet had resumed its grip on the rock, but only feebly. When the tide came back in, the waves might knock it off, and whirl it round and smash it . . . He felt somehow terribly, terribly guilty and wished he hadn't done it. But he could never resist, till afterwards.

The dog barked impatiently, summoning him on, not understanding why he was wasting the wonderful morning. He scrambled on after it, trying to stop worrying about the limpet.

*

They came round Castle Cliff at last, safe into King Edward's Bay. Little, snug, a sun-trap his dad had called it, when they came down for the day before the war. Chock-full of bathers then, deck-chairs, ice-cream kiosks and places where you could get a tray of tea for a shilling, and a shilling back on the crockery afterwards.

Not now. Totally empty.

And divided into two halves by the wire; huge rolls of barbed wire, stretching like serpents from cliff to cliff. Inland of the wire, the beach was dead mucky, full of footmarks, dropped fag-ends, rusting, broken bits of buckets and spades. People still came here for a smell of the briny, even in wartime. Holidays-at-home ... the government organized it ... fat girls in their pre-war frocks, dancing with each other in the open air on the Prom, to the music of the local army band in khaki uniform; pretending they were having a hell of a good time, and hoping one of the band would pick them up afterwards ...

Seawards of the wire, the beach was clean, smooth, pure, washed spotless by the outgoing tide. Sometimes the waves, at the highest tides, passed through the wire. Nothing else did. For there were notices with a skull and crossbones, warning of the minefields buried under the sand to kill the invading Jerries, or at least blow their legs off.

Unfortunately, the dog could not read. It went straight up to the wire and began to wriggle through, waggling its hips like a girl trying to catch a soldier's eye. Brian shouted at the dog, leaping up and down, frantic. Feeling responsible, feeling he'd brought it here. Forgetting *it* had brought *him*.

The dog took no notice. It finished its wriggling and leapt gaily on to the clean, wet, flat sand. It became sort of drunk with space and wetness and flatness, tearing round in ever-increasing circles, cornering so sharply its feet slid and it nearly fell on its side. Brian waited terrified for the small savage flash and explosion, braced to see large, furry, bloody bits of dog fly through the air, as if they were legs of pork in a butcher's shop before the war.

But nothing happened. The dog changed its tactics and began dive-bombing bits of wreckage that were strewn about, leaping high in the air, and coming down hard with all four feet together. Throwing things up in the air and catching them.

Why didn't the mines go off? That dog was as heavy as a grown man . . . Then Brian looked at the sand under the wire. There were all sizes of dog-tracks running through it. The dogs of the town had obviously found out something the humans didn't know.

There were no mines. The army couldn't afford them. All they could afford were notices warning of mines. Then the people who read them would think they could sleep safe in their beds at night, thinking the mines were protecting them from the Germans.

Fakes. Like the fake wooden anti-aircraft guns that Tommy Smeaton had found up the coast towards Blyth, guarded by a single sentry against the English kids who might wreck them. Fakes, like the airfields full of plywood Spitfires that kids played in round the Firth of Forth . . .

Brian didn't know whether to laugh or cry.

Then he followed the dog through the wire. Ran round in circles with it, teasing it with a long lump of seaweed. Jumped up and down expecting, still, with a strange half-thrill that there would be a bang under his feet at any moment, and he would go sailing through the air . . .

No bangs. He sat down breathless, and all that happened was that the damp sand soaked through the seat of his shorts.

When he got his breath back, he began to explore along the tide-line. Oh, glory, what a haul! A sodden sheepskin boot with a zip down the front, obviously discarded by a pilot who'd had to ditch in the sea. And it was a size seven, and the seven had a strange crossbar on it, which meant it was continental. A German pilot's boot!

Then he found a dull brown tin that clearly said it contained ship's biscuits. Iron rations, floated from the lifeboat of some sunken ship! British, so not poisoned, like people said German things were. He'd take them home to Mam.

A cork life-jacket, good as new. Oh, glory, what a place for war souvenirs, and not a kid in the whole town must know about it! A near-new shaving-brush for Dad ... German or British, it didn't matter. Dad's old one was pre-war, and nearly worn down to a stump.

His shirt-front began to bulge like a lady who was having a baby. Sea-water ran down under his belt, down the front of his shorts, but he didn't care. A brier pipe, an aluminium pan without a dent, a good broom-head, a lovely silver-backed mirror. He had his pockets stuffed, his hands full, things tucked under both armpits so he could hardly walk. In the end he had to make dumps of useful stuff, every few yards above the tide-line. He couldn't carry them all home at once; he must hide some, bury some in the dry sand and come back for it later.

The last find took his breath away. A violin in its case. The strings had gone slack; no sound came when he twanged them, but surely it must be worth a bob or two? Dad would know.

He moved on into sudden shadow. He looked up, and saw that he was nearly at the foot of the far cliff. Where the Mermaid's Cave was.

Nobody called it the Mermaid's Cave but him. He had found it in the last year of peace. There was nothing in it but a long floor of wet, glistening pebbles, full of the smell of the sea. But each pebble glowed wonderfully in the blue-lit gloom. It was a miraculous place; the kind of place you might expect to find a mermaid . . . if anywhere on earth.

Not that, at thirteen, he believed in mermaids any more. Only in soppy poems they taught you at junior school. 'The Forsaken Merman.' Hans Christian Andersen's 'Little Mermaid'. And his cousin George's RAF joke, about what are a mermaid's vital statistics . . . 38–22–1/6d. a pound!

But he wished there *were* mermaids. He had a daydream about coming into the cave and surprising one, combing her long blonde hair down to half conceal her rosy breasts, like in fairy-tale books or the photos from the Windmill Theatre. It would be nice to . . . his mind always sheered away from what it would be nice to do with her.

Ah, well. No mermaids now. Just war souvenirs. You couldn't have everything, and already today had been better than Christmas. Still, he'd look inside, like he always had. Might be a lump of Jerry aeroplane or something . . .

There was *something*. Something long and pale, stretched out. Almost like a person lying there . . .

Barmy! Things always changed into something else, when you walked right up to them boldly. But that could almost be a long leg, a long bare leg, as shapely as the girls' at the Windmill.

He shot upright so hard, he banged his head painfully on the rock roof. But when he opened his eyes after the agony, she was still there. The Mermaid. Her hair was gracefully swirled across the pebbles, the way the sea had left her. Her wide grey eyes were looking straight at him, with an air of appeal. Her face was pale, but quite untouched. She'd been wearing a dress, but there wasn't that much left of it. Just enough to pass the censors at the Windmill.

Transfixed, he slowly reached out and touched her. Her face was cold. Not human cold, like when somebody comes in from a winter's day, or has been bathing. No, she was as cold as a vase full of flowers. As cold as a thing that is not alive.

Dead. But death and the sea had been kind to her; and to him. Nothing had touched her except the thing that had killed her. If there had been blood, the sea had washed it away on her voyage ashore. She was dead, but she was entirely beautiful. She was beautiful, but entirely dead. On the beautiful pebbles of the cave, with her hair around her. No smell but the clean smell of the sea. She might have been a lovely ship's figure-head, washed ashore after a shipwreck.

He just stood and stared and stared. She must have come off some ship. What was she? Norwegian, Dutch, Danish? Sometimes their coasters carried the captain's wife and family.

He was there a long time. Somehow he knew that once he moved, nothing would ever be the same again. She would change into something else, like the piece of wood that wasn't a bird; like the minefield that wasn't really a minefield.

He would have liked to take her home.

He would like to have kept her here, and come to see her often.

But he was a realist in the end. He remembered the cods' heads on the rocks. Once he moved, they would put her in a hole in the ground. Once he moved, she would only exist on a written form. And she was so beautiful, here in her cave . . .

He might have stayed . . . how long? But he heard the roar of the waves; the roar of the returning tide. He ran out in a panic. Waves were starting to stream up the beach, and the dog was nowhere to be seen.

He began to run up the beach. There was a khaki-clad figure on the cliff, striding to and fro on sentry-duty. Brian waved and shouted, and then began to cry as he ran.

He had no idea why he was crying. All the rest of his life, he could never quite work out why he had been crying.

After the Funeral

There's only one British plane flying over Germany at night, and that's a BA 146, the quietest jet in the world. That's why the Federal Republic tolerates it – Bonn is very fussy about its citizens enjoying unbroken sleep; keeps them placid, law-abiding little Germans.

The 146 is an express-parcels plane run for TNT, the Rupert Murdoch crowd who took such a lot of flak at Wapping. Unlike Wapping, the flight's as quiet as the grave. No passengers, no cabin crew, just the captain and first officer and a lot of dark empty air over Germany.

I know all this, because I fly it most nights. It's such a doddle it's hard to keep awake. You have the German air-traffic control nearly all to yourself, and they're good and reliable and clear. You don't have to worry about near-misses in the air, like approaching Prestwick, or over Greece in the holiday season.

A graveyard shift, so it's important to have a nice lively first officer to keep you awake. Like Fairhurst was, when I flew to Majorca for Britannia. Fairhurst used to spend his spare time practising balancing a small light-bulb in the upward stream of warm air from the gasper. He practised so long he could get it to balance perfectly; just hang in

the air, motionless. Then he'd summon the senior air-
hostess and kid her the damned light-bulb hovering there
was a new and infallible lie-detector. She'd fall for it
usually. Then he'd start to question her about what she'd
been up to, and who with, the previous night. A riot, that
would keep us happy right across France. Bright lad,
Fairhurst. He'll do well, if he survives to maturity . . .

Unfortunately, I no longer had Fairhurst. Most nights I
got Stringer. Now I don't want to knock Stringer. A decent
lad, and a thoroughly painstaking first officer. Not the sort
to get aboard with a hangover and pull up the flaps in a fit
of abstraction while you're still trying to gain height. But
his idea of a rave-up is stamp-collecting. When you're in
foreign parts for the night, he can never let his hair down
– he's like a good little schoolboy who thinks the Head's
always watching. It's hard even to get him out of uniform,
whereas most of us can't wait to get out of our monkey-
suits. A child of older parents . . .

The night I'm talking about, he was especially bad.
We'd no sooner taken off and climbed up through Manchester Control to our cruising altitude of 24,000 feet,
heading for Pole Hill VOR-beacon, when I realized there
was something really wrong with him. Soggy as a drowned
hamster. Not one inessential word could I get out of him;
not even about stamp-collecting. I looked across to where
he was sitting in the right-hand seat. The dim white light
from the instruments wasn't exactly penetrating, but I
could see pretty dark shadows under his eyes. I thought I'd
better get him to talk. In a cabin not much bigger than a
toilet-cubicle, bad vibes can get pretty lethal on a long
flight.

'Got gut-ache?'

'No ... no.' He was silent for a long minute, then seemed to think he owed me some sort of explanation.

'It was my father's funeral, yesterday.'

Talk about a conversation-stopper. But you have to say something. 'How old was he?' I don't know why everybody always says that. I suppose they're hoping the deceased was about ninety-seven. As if being ninety-seven makes it any better.

'Sixty-three.'

We flew on in that awful silence.

'Had he been ill long?' Another stupid question, but you *have* to say something.

'He wasn't ill. He went out with a shotgun and blew his head off.'

Even I could think of nothing to say to that. Luckily, we were just reaching Pole Hill and the fuss of turning for Otringham, the next beacon near Hull. I suppose I hoped in a cowardly way that the interruption would change the subject. But Stringer, having got started, was obviously going on.

'It's my mother I feel sorry for. He led her a hell of a dance all their married life. Brooding for weeks on end; not speaking a word. Then he'd get these sudden black rages. Couldn't hold any sort of job down, for years. My mother had to go out to work, to keep things going. At least it got her out of the house.'

'What did he do – when he was working?'

'He was in the RAF in the war. With BEA after that, flying Yorks. Then he flew a desk. That was the one thing I ever did that pleased him – learning to fly. He liked to talk to me about my flying.'

The silence got really massive after that. I took refuge in

looking out of the cabin window. It was a glorious moonlit night, without a cloud in the sky. We were just crossing the coast. The whole Humber Estuary was laid out like a map, as they say in books. The sea shone under the moon like beaten pewter. We were turning a bit now, heading for an imaginary point in the North Sea known as Dogger.

'A pointless bloody life,' said Stringer, 'and a pointless bloody death. Pity he didn't do it years ago, then my mother could've found somebody nicer.'

He was almost talking to himself by this time. Not a happy sensation, being cooped up at 24,000 feet with a guy who was talking to himself. I just hoped he wasn't going to do anything embarrassing, like cry. Let alone something dangerous. I didn't think he would. Got the stiff upper lip, has old Stringer.

More's the pity perhaps. He was damming it all up inside. We flew on in a silence that got denser and denser, full of electricity building up, like inside a bank of cu-nimbus. If you've ever had the misfortune to fly through a bank of cu-nimbus clouds, you'll know what I mean. A big bank of cu-nimbus can tear an aircraft to bits in seconds. You fly in one side, and you don't come out the other.

It was a relief when we reached Dogger, half-way across the North Sea, and it was time to transfer to Maastricht Control in Holland. The controller had a good stolid Dutch voice, which I clung to like a drowning man to a life-raft. Somewhere out there were ordinary Dutch humans. Windmills, daffodils and tulips, pretty girls in fancy dress offering you bits of Gouda cheese, and much more if you got lucky. The Dutchman spoke in English, of course; all air-traffic controllers do, even the Greeks try to. The Dutch are hard to tell from the Germans, but occasionally the Dutch make ponderous, boring little jokes. The Germans never do; it would not be *korrekt*.

It was at that point that the first odd thing happened, though it didn't seem very odd at the time. It was just a strong smell of leather. Real sweaty leather. Much lived-in leather. Like when you stand next to a motorcyclist in a Chinese takeaway.

I knew it wasn't coming from me. I glanced at Stringer. He sat there, as immaculate as ever in his white shirt and tie. He'd never smelt of anything worse than Denim after-shave before. Perhaps under the burden of bereavement, he'd forgotten to change his socks . . .

I don't want to sound carping, but that sort of thing matters when you're in a tiny pressurized space. Little things mean a lot, in the wrong sort of way. I once had a first officer who whistled television jingles under his breath when he was concentrating. He didn't even know he was doing it. By the end of a five-hour flight, I felt like pulling out the control column by the roots and braining him with it.

Still, this wasn't the night to say anything to Stringer. He had enough to put up with.

But the damned smell didn't go away, even after I'd turned the air-conditioning right up. It got stronger, rottener. And there was another acrid smell now; an old-fashioned smell right out of my childhood . . . Carbolic. What they used in school toilets. And, in fact, in other ways the whole cockpit was starting to smell like the worst kind of school toilet.

I was relieved to see, glancing sideways, that Stringer's nostrils were working as well.

'Something wrong with the bog?' he said.

'Go and check.'

The bog in the 146 is just behind the flight deck, and about as big as a large suitcase. I am always amazed at the ingenuity of those who design aircraft bogs. Never was so much crammed into so little for the use of so many. As a place, it didn't take long to check.

'Clean as a whistle,' I heard Stringer say behind my head. 'Smells like a rose. Wherever it's coming from, it's not coming from here.'

'Maybe there's a dead ferret trapped in with the nose-wheel,' I said. But neither of us laughed.

When Stringer got back into his seat, he went on sniffing. 'I can smell petrol too.' Which was just plain stupid. The 146 runs on kerosene, like any other jet. The only petrol you get in a jet is in the pilot's cigarette-lighter.

But he was right. The whole cabin was reeking of petrol, like a car with a leaking tank.

I looked at Stringer, and Stringer looked at me. We both had the same thought; the parcels behind us. Maybe some Arab terrorist was giving us an early Christmas present. I got up and checked the parcels myself; they just smelt of cardboard.

'Oil pollution at sea?' suggested Stringer. 'Coming in through the air-intakes?'

It seemed a bit unlikely at 24,000 feet.

Then the smells just went away. We sniffed and sniffed, but there was only Stringer's Denim aftershave, as usual. So we forgot it. Just one of those things.

Then we had something else to worry about. A little burst of vibration through the airframe; then another, then a third. Stringer started sniffing. 'Smells like Guy Fawkes night . . .'

He was right. It was just as if some fool had let off a firework in the cabin. For a second I had the illusion that the cabin was full of smoke.

But in a second, it was gone again.

We flew on, waiting for the vibration to come again; wondering whether to get the plane down, and fast. But she flew on without a flaw.

'It didn't feel like real trouble,' said Stringer. 'All the dials are reading OK.'

Oddly enough, I agreed with him. You get lots of funny little vibrations when you're flying that you can never explain. But they don't kill you. I decided to fly on. Once you divert from a flight, there's endless admin. hassle. TNT don't like parcels arriving late, and there are bloody awful forms to fill in.

'Coast coming up.'

From our height you could see it all: from the German islands round Borkum in the north, to the many mouths of the Rhine, the Maas and Waal to the south. Like black embroidery on silver lace.

'Hey,' said Stringer, 'the coast looks different.'

It did. There seemed to be a hole in it, where the old Zuyder Zee used to be. The Dutch drained their inland sea after the war – turned it into farmland, the polders, behind high dikes. Where once fishing-boats had sailed, tulips now grew. One of the seven new wonders of the world.

But it looked for all the world as if, tonight, the dykes had burst and the sea flooded back, drowning the farms under the waves.

'There was nothing about it on the ten o'clock news,' said Stringer. 'I think it must be low-lying mist, over the polders.'

'Yeah,' I said. I had enough to think about, without what was going on 24,000 feet beneath me.

Then he said, 'It's odd, that's all. That's how the Zuyder Zee must've looked when my father flew over it.'

'Ah, well, not our problem.' I was just relieved he was talking about his father in a more normal voice.

You're always afraid it might happen; you never stop watching out for it. But when it does happen, it's still like a 20,000-volt electric shock running through your muscles.

A near-miss. One hell of a near-miss. One minute we were sailing along through clear air, and the next there was this black plane only fifty feet in front.

Thank God it was heading away from us; thank God we were only slowly overtaking it.

I went into a dive to the left before I knew it. I shall never forget the way it hung over us, the great black wing, with the semi-circles of four whirling prop-blades beneath it. Then it was gone. I straightened up, near-rigid with shock. 'What the hell *was* it?'

Stringer took out a very white handkerchief and mopped his face. 'Four engines,' he said. 'Prop job. Twin tail. No navigation lights.' Then it seemed to hit him. 'The crazy bastard was flying without navigation lights . . .'

When I got my wits back, I gave the controller at Maastricht what for, in no uncertain terms. If another Anglo-Dutch War ever breaks out, blame me.

He was maddeningly calm and smug, like the Dutch usually are. 'There is no aircraft within fifty miles of you . . .'

'You want to get yourself a new radar, chum!'

'There is nothing wrong with my radar. I see you quite clearly. You are too low. Please climb 500 feet . . .'

'I'm reporting it as a near-miss . . .'

'You must do what you think best. Please climb back to 24,000.'

I vowed inwardly to fix him in the morning, and shut up. There is no point in getting them upset; that way you cut your own throat. We flew on, drinking coffee and trying to get over it, at least so our hands would stop shaking.

'Look at that stuff over at three o'clock,' said Stringer. I gave a quick glance to starboard. As you can imagine, my mind was strictly on what might be straight ahead, so I didn't pay much attention to what was silhouetting his dark profile. But I remember there were a lot of searchlights waving about, mostly that slightly yellowish-white, but there was one distinctly blue and much thinner than the rest. The spectacular thing, though, was the fireworks. Green clusters hanging motionless in the sky, which must have been attached to parachutes, and a lot of red and yellow stuff, moving in slow arcs.

'Must be a festival,' I said. 'Queen Juliana's birthday or something . . .'

'It's not Juliana now,' he said. 'She abdicated. It's her daughter. I can't remember her name.'

'Well, somebody's birthday,' I said. 'Somebody important. There's the same sort of thing going on over Arnhem, on my side.'

'But some of that stuff's going up to 20,000 feet. That's downright bloody dangerous to aircraft.'

'Well, it's not at 24,000. That's all I care about.'

'And it's after midnight . . .'

'Look, just concentrate. Time we switched to Rhein.'

I thanked Maastricht, without any warmth creeping into my voice, and got the sober Teutonic tones of the

Rhein controller that promised no messing about. We turned to starboard slightly, now flying towards Dortmund beacon. I wasn't sorry to say goodbye to Holland; all Holland seemed a bit spooky, kinky, off-key that night. It happens sometimes, but you're always glad when it's over. Change your controller, change your luck.

We flew on over that quiet dark bit, between the Dutch border and the Ruhr. It calmed me, but Stringer continued twitchy.

'There aren't any street-lights down there.'

'For Christ's sake, it's after midnight . . .'

'There's always street-lights. There weren't any street-lights over Holland, either . . .'

'Must be your bloody ground-mist, drifting off the Zuyder Zee.' To tell you the truth, I wasn't paying much attention to his babbling on. I was fed up with him; I was fed up with the whole trip. Roll on, Frankfurt!

'Anyway,' I added, 'there's plenty of light over the Ruhr.'

There was too. A great dim mass of light, reaching far into the sky far ahead. It did strike me it wasn't quite the usual colour. It's usually yellow, from the sodium lamps. This was a fiery pink.

'Freak weather conditions.' I got the Frankfurt *Volmet* weather-computer on our second radio.

No ground mist over Frankfurt. None anywhere over the Ruhr. I remember how clear the recorded voice was; no static or interference. So it was a bit of a shock when the other voice broke in, blurred and full of static. A German voice, speaking German. Then another German voice replied, speaking German.

They were talking to each other, and in spite of the

static and the foreign language, it was definitely an aircraft talking to its controller. I haven't got much German, but I could make out the word *Libelle* – Dragonfly. Dragonfly control to Dragonfly. The quality of transmission was pathetic, like an old scratched 78 gramophone record. As a pilot, it gave me the heebie-jeebies.

'Who the hell is that on the air?' Stringer nearly yelped, and I didn't blame him. Your controller is your lifeline. Some other silly bastard blocking up the airwaves, you could end up dead. Not at 24,000 over Germany at night, of course. But on the run-in to landing at Frankfurt . . .

The voices came again. Something about a *kurier* flying at 22,000, and steering a course 105 to intercept.

'Sounds like the German Air Force – sounds like some sort of night-fighter exercise, using the wrong frequency.'

We told Rhein. Rhein was positive and reassuring. Rhein had heard none of it. There was no German Air Force exercise scheduled for that night. Which means, to the Teutonic mind, that it can't possibly exist . . .

I tried to console myself that Dragonfly and his control had by now shut up. Maybe they could take a hint. Maybe they knew they'd dropped a clanger and had buggered off quietly, hoping they wouldn't be reported in the morning. It seemed to me I was going to report half of Europe in the morning. Maybe I was getting stroppy in my old age.

'What on earth *is* that ahead?' asked Stringer in an awed voice. And I must admit it was odd. The pink glow ahead had got much bigger. It was still blurred, but it seemed to be filling the horizon now, as if the whole bloody Ruhr was on fire.

That was the last sane thought I had for half an hour. Because suddenly another voice came through our headphones. An English voice; a cockney voice; a voice hoarse with excitement. No, to be frank, a voice shit-scared, babbling.

'Rear-gunner to skipper. Corkscrew. Corkscrew right.'

The plane just seemed to go bananas under my hands. The right wing dropped until it was pointing at the ground. We fell in a sickening dive. There was the sound of something like a dustbin breaking loose in the compartment behind. All the evil smells came back with a rush, and overpowering all, a strong smell of shit. Then both the voices together. Dragonfly yelling he had the *kurier* in his sights, in German. And the cockney voice shouting, 'Corkscrew left, skipper. Corkscrew left,' in a high-pitched scream.

Then little vibrations the same as we'd had before. Then a much heavier vibration; a really nasty vibration, as if the 146 was in some way damaged. The smell of fireworks. The smell of rubber burning. A terrifying roar of engines, old prop-job engines, totally deafening.

Then the cockney yelling, 'I got him skip. I got him. He's burning.' With a kind of savage, screaming exultation that made you feel sick. Or was it the way the 146 was falling around? I knew the 146 couldn't take that kind of bashing. Any minute it would break up . . .

Then, before I could gather my wits even to move the controls and try to get the plane upright . . .

Nothing.

The 146 was flying on over Germany, level and the right way up, as if nothing had ever happened.

No noise, no smell, no vibration. Rhein control broke in calmly, if a little reprovingly. Telling me to maintain my correct flying altitude by climbing 300 feet.

I obeyed, automatically, and got his approval, as if I was a small but beloved pupil.

I glanced over at Stringer, who hadn't said a word. He didn't turn towards me, like he normally does. He just said, in a dreamy voice that didn't sound like him at all,

'That was close, skipper.'

'What the hell do you mean?' I shouted. His voice scared me; it sounded like he was an actor, taking a part in a different play.

He didn't reply. At least he didn't reply to my question. He just said,

'Big fires ahead. The PFs must have got their markers down right for once.'

I became convinced I was going mad. Or I was in some horrible dream, and really safe back in England, in my bed at the Birmingham Holiday Inn.

Because, where Frankfurt airfield should have been, and Rhein control, there was just fire. Fire that spread out mile after mile. Fire that shot in towering pillars fifteen thousand feet into the air. A fire that seemed to breathe like a giant obscene living animal, crouching over a Germany that was its prey.

Another voice; another voice like a cracked 78 gramophone record came through my headphones.

'Five minutes to ETA, skip. Commence bomb-run.'

And another strange voice, slightly Scottish this time. 'Left a bit, skip. Left a bit more . . . right a bit.'

But my hands didn't move on the control-column. I was paralysed with sheer fright, because just ahead of us, outlined against the flames, the black four-engined plane was back. And between its twin-fins was a bulbous, shiny, glass object with four black sticks jutting out that could only be a gun-turret.

I knew from my time in the Air Training Corps what kind of plane it was. I had seen it doing a fly-past on Battle of Britain Sunday.

A Lancaster bomber of World War II.

And not just one Lancaster. There were dozens of them, flying almost wing-tip to wing-tip, jostling each other like kids queuing up for ice-cream at the cinema, rising and falling as the updraughts of air from the fires below hit and lifted them.

And far below us, crucifixes against the roaring, breathing beast of flame that was the Ruhr, flew other four-engined bombers with long bodies and short stubby wings. As I watched one of them suddenly gave a bright flash, and lost a whole two-engined wing, and fell twisting away into the inferno.

'Poor bloody Stirlings are copping it tonight,' said Stringer in his ghastly dreamy voice. Like a living puppet.

And I was like a puppet myself, hands rigid on the control-column. Because I knew I must not move it. To move it would be to go for ever into that nightmare that Stringer was already caught up in. Move it, and we would end up in some inferno of our own. For the world outside and the world inside didn't fit. My dials said I was flying at 400 knots, whereas the Lancasters outside my windscreen couldn't possibly be doing more than 280 on full boost. I was literally flying blind. In that heat and that stink, and with that inferno outside, only my own instruments were real.

I seemed to fly on forever.

And then, breaking through like a cool clear stream of

water, the voice of the Rhein controller, asking slightly querulously when I would be starting my descent, and what was my intended vector? His voice sort of broke up the whole scene, and I was back in the cool dark at 24,000 feet over Germany.

Frankly, I don't know how I got locked on to the ILS beam and got my glide-slope. My body felt like soggy elastic; my hands shook like I'd developed Parkinson's. I was sitting in a puddle of my own sweat. And Stringer was still locked in his dream, babbling to a non-existent radio-operator about checking possible damage to the main spar . . .

But I did it. It wasn't the best landing I've ever made, but I didn't bend anything. And I managed to taxi in the right direction once I was on the ground. I don't think anybody noticed anything . . .

Then I only had the simple job of coping with a totally lunatic first officer before the German ground-crew got to us. But Stringer wasn't mad any more, at least he wasn't babbling. He just sat there in his seat, tears streaming down his face, saying over and over again,

'Sorry, Dad. Sorry, sorry, sorry. I just didn't understand.'

I told the Germans he'd been taken ill, just as we were about to land. Severe headache and abdominal cramps. Some German medics took him away on a stretcher.

They sent him home after a whole week, saying they couldn't find a thing wrong with him. Thorough types, the Hun. I kept my mouth shut, and he didn't lose his licence. He took a short-haul job after that, flying Islanders to the Hebrides. By daylight. As far as I know, he's still doing it without any evil result. Still, I worry about him; and the Islanders.

After the Funeral

I checked up on the quiet with RAF records. Wing-commander Stringer, DSO, DFC and bar, flew eighty-nine operations in Lancasters and was demobbed from the RAF in October 1945.

I'm just glad I never had a father like that.

Zakky

Dad's Army?

I'll bet it made you laugh. But none of it was true, not round where I lived.

That rubbish about drilling with pitchforks and broom handles. Every lad in our village had his own shotgun by sixteen; been using one since he was ten. They could drop a half-grown rabbit at a hundred yards. What else d'you think they lived on? Farm-labourers' wages? All the government had to do was issue shot-gun cartridges containing one big solid shot, which would have blown a hole in Jerry big enough to put your hand through.

We had five gamekeepers in our lot; knew every spinney and gap in the hedge for miles. And twice as many poachers, fly enough to swipe the Lady Amherst pheasants off the terrace of Birleigh Manor, while his lordship sat there drinking afternoon tea. Brutal men, all of them. I've known some stagger home needing sixteen stitches in their head after some little encounter in the dark. They made peace while they were on Home Guard duty, and went back to their private war afterwards.

Yes, we did have a poet. Laurie Tomlinson. Professor somewhere now. But then he'd just got back from the

Spanish Civil War. Showed us how to garrotte a man with a piece of piano wire so he died without a sigh. Showed the village blacksmith how to make a two-inch mortar from a yard of steel gas-piping. The army took those off us later, saying they were too dangerous to use. But they fired mortar-bombs all right; the ones Pincher Morton pinched from the Polish camp down the road.

And we never drilled in pinstripe suits or cricket shirts. We never wasted time drilling at all. We went on patrol in the washed-out browns and greys that poachers wore, which blend with the woodland at five paces. Laurie taught us how to put boot-polish on our faces so that it didn't crack and drop off like mud. Our village poachers still use boot-polish . . .

And, poachers or not, they were all old *soldiers*. From the Last Lot. Hard-bodied farmhands of forty, who'd been snipers in the mud of the Somme, or bomb-throwers in the Ypres Salient. When we finally got our old Canadian rifles, dating from 1912, they nursed them like grim mothers. Very anxious to get their hands on the bayonets. First they sharpened them on their own whetstones, then they blackened them so no glint would give away their position.

All the young lads were mad to join. The veterans wouldn't have 'em. War wasn't for kids, they said. Forgetting they'd been little more than kids themselves in the Last Lot. We only ever had two young 'uns in our platoon. I was one.

I'd tried for a commission in our county regiment. Then for the R A F as anything. Even the navy, though I was seasick crossing to the Isle of Wight. But I had flat feet. When I put any weight on my feet, my toes pointed up in the air like ac-ac guns. Didn't count that I played rugger, and ran cross-country. I was *out*.

Went to see Major Newsam; asked if he'd pull a few strings for me with his old mates. He shook his head and told me the best thing I could do was to farm the land my father had left me as well as I damned well could. Damned U-boats would try to starve the country out, just like the Last Lot.

As a sop, he let me join his Home Guard. As second-in-command, with a pip on my shoulder.

'Old soldiers need someone to look up to,' he said. 'Someone to look after. Leave all the organizing to your platoon-sergeant. Never ask a man to do what you can't do yourself.'

It was a rule he kept himself, even though he'd lost half an arm in Iraq in 1924.

When they asked for Draggett's Mill as their HQ, I couldn't refuse. Right in the middle of my land; on the highest hill for miles, to make the best of the wind. But Draggett had been gone a long time, and the mill was just an empty stone shell, like a squat, blackened milk-bottle. They fitted it out with new floors and ladders, and with a parapet of sandbags and a corrugated iron roof, it made an ideal look-out for German paratroopers dropping in.

It was there, as we stood-to one lovely soft summer evening in 1940, that they dragged Zakky in. They'd caught him following them, and they thought he was a German spy. He'd put up a hell of a fight; three of them were bleeding. They'd had to knock him senseless with a rifle-butt. They poured water over him from our brew-up milk- churn, and he opened one swollen eye a green slit and said,

'*English!* If you had been Germans, I would have killed you all.'

'Nasty little sod, sir,' said Curly Millbank. 'He had this hidden under his shirt, at the back of his neck.' He passed me a simple flat knife, honed to a needle point.

'Give me my knife!' The thin wet figure on the floor came at me so fast he knocked me clean across the trestle table that served as our office. All knees and elbows he was, and they felt as sharp as needles too. It took four of them to drag him off me, and somebody else got bitten.

'Who are you?' I asked, when I'd got my breath back.

'I am *soldier*.' He drew himself up to his full five foot three. 'Zbigniew Zakrewski, Polish Army.' He gabbled some long number. 'They give me a number. They had no rifles.'

'I think I've seen him hanging round the Polish camp, sir,' said Pincher Morton. 'The soldiers feed him. But he's not one of them.'

Zakky pulled a horrible face. 'I go to them. Tell them how to kill Nazis. They make me peel spuds.' He spat on our highly polished floor. 'That is why I follow your men. I will show *you* how to kill Nazis.'

He drew his hand across his throat.

Major Newsam came in then, and took over. I was still feeling a bit shaken.

'Checked up on him with the Poles,' Newsam told me at stand-to next evening. 'He's Polish all right. Thirteen years old. Joined the Polish Army in their retreat last September. Never had a rifle, never had a uniform. Marched five days, then met the Russkis coming the other way. Got away when the rest surrendered. Seems to have sneaked out through the Balkans and stowed away on a ship from Piraeus. Lot of Poles came that way. The Polish Government in exile tried putting him in a children's home, but he just kept running away. Apparently he eats at the Polish camp and sleeps in the woods. Keeps trying to nick weapons from their armoury. They're terrified he'll end up doing somebody an injury. I mean, all the Poles are fighting-mad, but he's got even them scared *silly*. They asked if I could get somebody to adopt him . . .' He looked at me queryingly. 'Think your mother could take him on?'

Old Newsam was a bit sweet on my mother; thought she was wonder-woman.

I looked him straight in the eye. 'You'll have to bribe him. Let him join the Home Guard . . .'

He grinned and said, 'Pity about your flat feet, Keith. You wouldn't have made a bad officer, given time.'

So I drove him home in my old farm van, the scruffy little tick. He ponged out the van to high heaven. When we got home, I heard my mother playing the piano. Chopin. She used to work like hell all day: the farm, evacuees, W V S, the lot. But when she was finally done for the day, she still liked to get dressed up a bit, and have a drink, and light the tall thin brass candles that stood on the piano, and play Chopin. Said it convinced her there'd be a better world again, some day.

I was going to march straight in and interrupt her, because I wanted to get back to the mill in case anything had happened while I'd been gone. But, in the half-open doorway, a small, steely hand caught my wrist. And Zakky just stood there till she had finished, the tears running down his cheek in the candle-light. It was the Chopin, I suppose.

When she had finished, and turned and smiled at us, he went straight up to her, clicked his heels together, and gave a funny little bow of his head. He was such an odd little scruff, I wondered how even a woman as wise as my mother would take it. But she took it all in her stride, shook him by the hand, and asked him if he'd care for a bath?

So I left her to get on with it. The next morning he came down to breakfast in one of my old grey school suits, white shirt and tie, long dark hair slicked down with tap water. Apparently she'd laid out the suit and shirt next to his pathetic rags on his bed, while he had a bath, and he'd chosen freely to wear them. Only he'd asked her to wash the rags for him, because they were Polish and precious. (And she spent hours mending them, as well.) And he'd showed her a solid gold locket, with a photo of a fierce, moustached military man on one side, and a rather lovely dark-haired woman on the other.

'My father. My mother.' He had clicked his heels again.

'Where are they now, Zakky?'

'Dead,' he said and took the locket back, and he never showed it to anybody else, ever. She said it was the only thing he had, except for the throwing knife that he still wore at the back of his neck, under the grey English suit.

I studied him over the bacon and eggs. I think his family must have been pretty well off, back in Poland, because he had exquisite table manners, only a little strange and foreign. And though he had the body of a half-starved kid, his face was . . . ageless. Beaky nose, strong Polish cheekbones and a strong Polish jawbone, the sort you never see in an Englishman. His eyes were deep-sunken. They were either blazing with excitement, or too sad to look at direct.

They only blazed when he talked about Poland; or killing Nazis. Or when he was talking direct to my mother.

In his eyes, my mother could do no wrong. He always called her Madam Bosworth, whether she was there or not. I think he would have done anything for her, even died.

I think she could even have got him to go to our village school, when it reopened in September. But she hadn't the heart. She soon found he spoke excellent French, and they would prattle away for hours, faster than I could follow. She found he knew quite a lot of German too, but he would never speak it, even for her.

'German is language for pigs.' He also said 'Russian is language for pigs', so I suppose he had Russian as well. Neither of us could imagine him sitting at a desk among the village children.

Anyway, all his heart was set on killing Nazis. He was at the mill every spare hour. When he wasn't cleaning rifles (which he learnt quickly and did with incredible thoroughness), he was our look-out, following every vapour-trail in the sky, like a cat following the flight of birds. We found him some Home Guard overalls, nearly small enough. My mother took three inches off the leg. And we ordered him to stay at his post of duty on top of the mill, whatever happened. I think old Newsam was afraid of something nasty happening. It was the height of the Battle of Britain, and there were a lot of parachutes coming down during the daytime air-battles, and, thank God, the majority were Jerries. The farmhands of our platoon worked in the fields with their rifles at the ready. But any Jerries they rounded up, they always took straight down to the police-station in the next village. By tacit agreement, nobody ever brought a Jerry to the mill.

But Zakky certainly earned his keep. As he learnt to trust

us, he would bring in the weapons from his hidden caches in the woods. Two Bren guns we returned to the Poles; Newsam gave their CO a right rocket about the security of their armoury. But the rifles we kept, and the Mills bombs and mortar-bombs. With Jerry waiting just across the Channel, we weren't inclined to be over-generous.

And at stand-to and stand-down, we would gather in amazement to hear his impromptu lectures on how to kill Nazis. He had some incredible idea about electrocuting tank-crews with the fallen electric cables from tram-cars, but as the nearest trams were fifty miles away, in Piccadilly Circus, that wasn't much good. But we liked his idea about stretching a steel cable between two tree-trunks, to decapitate Nazi despatch riders. And he showed us how to make a Molotov cocktail that really worked. And explained how to feed petrol-soaked blankets into the tracks of tanks, and how to leap on tanks from behind and block up their periscopes with a handful of mud. From the way he explained it, I thought he'd really done that. So did old Newsam.

Zakky was good for us. Half our men saw war as charging with fixed bayonets across the sea of mud and shell-holes that was no man's land. The other half saw it as slinking through the bushes, taking pot-shots at Jerries as if they were pheasants.

Zakky had seen tanks. In action.

But the men never loved him; he never belonged. He accepted being called 'Old Zakky' with good grace. But he would never laugh, never take part in their jokes and horseplay. Jokes were a serious waste of time. And he could never bear to be touched. Once Curly Millbank grabbed him from behind in fun and ended up on his back with a sprained wrist, which put him off work for a week.

Then came 'Cromwell'. The codeword for 'Invasion Imminent'. We shouldn't have been told, but Newsam had mates at Southern Command.

At stand-to, the men took it silently, very silently. Only Pincher Morton said, 'So it's come, then.' Some asked permission to go and say goodbye to their wives, but Newsam said no. He didn't want a panic like in France, with refugees blocking the roads. There was no argument; they were old soldiers. They got on with it.

We half blocked the London road, rolling out the great cylinders of concrete. Then all we had to do was wait, and inspect the passes of any car or lorry that passed. And watch from the top of the mill, for Jerry paratroopers landing.

I was up there with Newsam and Zakky. Below, the men who weren't manning the road-block were huddled round our transport: two private cars and a farmer's motorized haycart. The men were smoking, but cupping their hands round the glowing ends. The night was moonlit through wispy cloud. A good night for spotting parachutes. Behind our backs, London was burning again, a pulsating pink glow in the sky.

'Think we can hold them, sir?' I only said it for something to say. It felt like the start of a rugger-match against a big rugger school: not much hope of winning, but wanting to put up a good show.

'If the army can hold them on the beaches, I think we can mop up any paratroops.'

'If?' I squeaked. 'Montgomery's Third Division's down there.'

'They've got no heavy stuff; they had to leave all their heavy stuff behind at Dunkirk. Hardly an anti-tank gun to bless themselves with, poor bastards. Hardly a heavy machine-gun . . .'

'So what are *we* supposed to do?'

'I expect we'd last about five minutes against tanks. But some of the men should get away into the woods. After that, it's up to them. Might as well go back to their wives; sniping won't stop an armoured column . . .'

'Oh,' I said again. Was 'oh' all I could find to say? I nodded down towards the hands cupped round cigarettes. 'Do *they* know that?'

'They know. Sorry to be a pessimist, Keith, on your first show. But I don't want you having any illusions.'

'We will kill Nazis!' said Zakky harshly, from across the observation platform. 'We will kill *many* Nazis!'

We both jumped; I think we had forgotten he was there. He came across and glared at us. I could see, in the moonlight, that he was trembling. Not with fear, I think. More like a whippet just before you unleash it against a rabbit.

'Many, many Nazis,' he said again, then went back on watch, turning his back on us. As if in disgust.

'That boy worries me,' muttered Newsam. 'Keep a tight rein on him. He's going to kill somebody before the night's out, if we're not careful. I wish we could send him home. But he'll just bugger off into the woods. Best here, where we can keep an eye on him.'

The waiting was appalling. The night was so still, except for the odd rumble or series of sharp cracks, ghosting down the warm night wind from London. The countryside

I loved lay on peacefully, under the dim moon. The black bulk of the church tower. Silver light gleaming on the huddled thatch of the village. The stooks of corn in my own top field, standing neat as guards on parade. We were too far west to be in the direct path of the Jerry bombers heading for London.

Then the phone rang. A man seen climbing through the window of Elm Cottage ... Newsam shot off in his old Morris, four riflemen jammed in with him.

They were back in ten minutes. Newsam settled again, elbows on the sandbags of the parapet.

'Well?' I asked, after a long silence. I saw his shoulders heave, and thought for a wild second that he was crying. Then he said with a snort,

'Bobby Finlayson in bed with Len Taylor's missis. We dragged them both out mother-naked. There'll be hell to pay in the morning.' He couldn't stop laughing.

We were busy after that. Impounded a lorry of black market meat on its way up to London. Caught a vicar with six rover-scouts, all looking for a place to die for their country. Two courting couples in lay-bys, tanks full of black-market petrol. One enterprising burglar, with a mixed bag of silver from Mottersdon Court.

'Had no idea there was so much night-life in the country!' snorted Newsam.

'*English!*' muttered Zakky darkly to himself. But all this dashing about did everyone a bit of good. It was better than hanging around. Every time they came back they were laughing over something.

And then, just before dawn, we had three phone-calls in rapid succession, and I was left alone on top of the mill with Zakky.

Zakky

Why was it then that we heard the sound of planes above the hazy moonlit clouds? And saw two parachutes sloping gently down, towards the wooded crest of Burrow's Hill, across our little valley.

While I was still dithering with shock, Zakky said 'Nazis' and was gone down the top ladder.

I suppose I should've done something intelligent, like phone for help. But I couldn't think of who to phone. Perhaps I should have run to the men manning the road-block, but they were a hundred yards away. So I stupidly left my post of duty and ran after him.

As I said before, I'd been a cross-country runner. But pound along in my hobnailed boots as I might, I couldn't catch up with Zakky. I had him in sight as far as the village, but in the cornfields beyond I lost him. I knew where the parachutes had fallen, roughly. I knew the short-cuts through the wood. But Zakky knew them even better than me . . .

Yet it seemed as though I had got to a parachute first. No sign of Zakky. The chute was caught up in a tree, like a great white rustling ghost. A dark figure dangled below, about four feet off the ground, helpless, silent. I ran up to it, pulling out my dad's old Webley revolver from its First World War leather holster. I didn't know what to expect. They told us that in Holland and Belgium the German paratroops came down disguised as policemen, vicars and nuns. But this one . . . as the body swung and turned in the breeze, I saw the round top of a flying helmet and the glint on goggles. The bulk of a sheepskin flying-jacket.

'Christ,' said the body suddenly, 'cut me down, for God's sake. This crotch-strap's nearly got me cut in half.' He did sound like he was in agony. And he had a very Welsh accent.

I got out my clasp-knife and climbed the tree and cut him down somehow. I suppose it never occurred to me that a Nazi might have a Welsh accent. Anyway, once he was free, he just fell in a heap on the ground.

The next thing he said was, 'You'd better go and find Stan – Stanislav – my gunner. His English isn't much cop – he's a Pole. I don't want some yokel lynching him for a Nazi.'

'Where'd he come down?'

'Over there, somewhere.' He pointed vaguely towards the edge of the wood.

I've never run so fast in all my life. But I was too late: I found Zakky crouching over a body.

'Is dead,' said Zakky, with a lot of satisfaction.

'He's one of ours,' I said numbly, staring down at the dim white face beneath the flying-helmet. 'He was called Stanislav. He was a Pole.'

There was a long and terrifying silence. It just went on and on and on. When I couldn't stand it any longer I said,

'There's another one down the hill. He's Welsh. I think they bailed out of their night-fighter. You'd better give me a hand getting him back to the mill.'

It helped, getting the pilot down off the hill. He was quite badly hurt, and we had to carry him between us, making a chair of our hands. It gave me something to do, instead of thinking about Zakky and the dead gunner. Then I had to get the ambulance out to us.

The Welshman asked about his gunner, and I told him the gunner was dead. He just closed his eyes and nodded; I suppose they were used to losing their mates. He was a Defiant pilot, and Defiants didn't have much luck in the Battle of Britain.

Then some daft bugger over Malbury way rang the church bells, meaning the Invasion had really started, and all hell broke loose, with civilians taking to the roads, trying to get away from the coast. And then suddenly it was dawn, and word slowly trickled through that bugger-all had happened anywhere, except an extra-big raid on London.

'Ah, well,' said Newsam, 'we live to fight again.'

'Nearly time to get the cows milked,' said Pincher Morton. 'No point goin' to bed now. Just makes you feel dopey.'

I drove Zakky home. Neither of us said a word. I didn't ask him how the gunner died; I couldn't bear to know. Maybe he just found him dead. I preferred to think that. Nothing I could do would bring the gunner back to life.

They came with a hearse and took the gunner's body away, later that morning. We never heard any more about it.

Then came October, with the equinoctial gales lashing up the Channel, and news that Hitler was dispersing his flat-bottomed barges at Boulogne. We were safe for the winter.

Newsam still drove us hard. He talked endlessly about *when* Hitler came in the spring. We trained more men; we were a full company now, four platoons and I was a platoon-commander. They built us pill-boxes of foot-thick concrete, and we trained with something called a Blacker Bombard that threw thermite-bombs at fake tanks made of corrugated iron which ran down a little railway outside Eastbourne. But somehow we couldn't *quite* believe in it; there was a feeling that Hitler had missed the boat.

All except Zakky, who grew grimmer than ever. He

made this huge plywood cut-out of a Nazi storm-trooper, advancing with a hideous grimace and a sub-machine-gun. Spent hours throwing his knife at it. I'd never believed in throwing-knives, couldn't see how they could even go through the cloth of a uniform. They were something you saw in the movies. But Zakky could throw from all angles and never missed, and I once tried levering his knife out of the thick plywood. It was embedded two inches, and I had a hell of a time getting it out. One or two of the platoon had narrow squeaks, coming across Zakky without warning when he was practising. It didn't make him any more loved. But he was something to talk about in the dull times, when we were out all night in the rain, and had nothing to show for it but the crew of some Jerry night-bomber, well soaked and ready to surrender for a mug of tea.

But we had to find him something to do, besides endlessly oiling rifles and throwing his knife at plywood. My mother got more and more worried about him. And the rabbits he brought back from the woods, always killed by his knife, did nothing to lessen her worries, though they helped out the rations.

Then came the blessed day that my new Fordson tractor broke down, only a week out of the factory. Furious, I rang Tom Hands the blacksmith, who fiddled with cars as a sideline.

That evening, when I got back from ploughing with our two old horses, the tractor was mended, and Tom and Zakky were in the kitchen with my mother, drinking tea from white enamel mugs, smirched with oily fingerprints. They were all as thick as thieves. Tom announced that Zakky had a gift with engines. My mother announced that

Tom was taking on Zakky as an apprentice. As spring broadened into summer, Tom and Zakky became inseparable. Worn-out farm machinery kept breaking down all over the place; they never had an idle moment.

And then Hitler invaded Russia, and we knew the threat from across the Channel was gone. To celebrate, Pincher Morton bought himself a plot in the village churchyard. Said he felt happier, knowing where he was going to end up.

We all felt happier; except Zakky. The further away the threat of invasion got, the blacker he became. You could feel the pressure building up in him. He was always wanting to *wrestle* with me. I took him on once or twice, in fun. Going gently, not wanting to hurt him, for I was a big lad by then, nearly fourteen stone.

He had me on my face in about ten seconds; somebody had taught him unarmed combat along the way. He never hurt me, but it was bloody humiliating. In the end I refused to do it any more, so he began jumping out on me from dark corners. Said I had to learn, for when the Nazis came.

But it wasn't the Nazis who came; it was the Canadians, whole divisions of them, armed to the teeth with American tanks and guns and lorries.

We had to pretend to defend the villages, while the Canadians pretended to attack them. Quite realistic, it was. Blank ammunition, thunderflashes, wired explosions, smoke-grenades. The trouble was, we were pretty good by then, and we knew the countryside. And they were so *green*; lousy soldiers who bunched up too close together, and stuck to the metalled roads. We ambushed and slaughtered them over and over again. Then they gave us fags and chewing-gum, grinning sheepishly. The battle-umpires kept running up and telling us *we* were dead, without giving any reasons. I don't think they wanted the Canadians to get too discouraged. Our old hands weren't too surprised when the Canadians finally got a bloody nose from real Germans, in the Dieppe Raid.

It was from one of these exercises that Zakky didn't come home. My mother and I were just setting out to look for him, in the van, when word came that Zakky was being held by the military. It seemed he had gone berserk and seriously injured a Canadian . . .

Major Newsam drove up to London, with my mother and the vicar. They must have talked bloody hard, because they brought Zakky back with them, paler and more silent, and blacker in his moods than ever.

Some weeks later, as we were getting ready for Christmas, the Japs attacked Pearl Harbor. In the New Year, we settled down to teaching the first American troops a thing or two.

All except Zakky.

The Americans were even more generous and clumsy than the Canadians had been. But, as Major Newsam said sadly, when we got our first issue of American tommy-guns, us Home Guard were all dressed up with nowhere to go. We were just actors now; the invasion threat had gone for ever. Still, we enjoyed the Camels and Hershey Bars.

Zakky was sixteen by then; as tall as he ever got, five feet seven. He shaved earlier than me, had a fine black moustache, whereas I could still get away with shaving twice a week. I suppose he was handsome in a thin, peaky, tragic sort of way. A lot of the local girls eyed him, even with the

Americans about. Rosemary Thomas, whose dad ran the White Lion, especially, though she was older than he was. I suppose the girls sensed the darkness in him; wanted to rescue him from it. But he had little time for them . . .

He was well in with the local farmers too. A natural mechanic, which was quite something in those days when we had to hold tractors together with tin cans and wire. I know he brought my mother's car back from the grave more than once, though he always insisted afterwards that she crawl underneath it, to be shown exactly what he'd done. He'd still do anything for her.

He even talked German now. Because she'd hit on a way of holding him steady. Soon, she told him, a great army would be invading Europe to fight the Nazis. They would need people who could speak French and German fluently . . . I think Major Newsam had something to do with that. He and my mother were as thick as thieves by that time. But I wasn't jealous. It was just nice to see two people I liked being happy.

They got married after harvest. October 1943. The whole village nearly went mad over it. We'd had a lot of wartime weddings, with blokes going off to the war, and people thinking they wouldn't come back. Desperate weddings, a kind of laughter on the edge of the grave. But my mother's wedding was different. It was, in a way, the first of our post-war weddings. People knew *they* were going to stay around and be married for the rest of their natural lives. There was no desperation in the laughter. We held the reception in the village hall, and the whole neighbourhood made a festival of it. They were both pretty popular with the locals and everyone chipped in with the eats, so we had a good spread in spite of the rationing. I gave my mother away in church and made a speech afterwards, which got a lot of laughs, Major Newsam being older than me, and my commanding officer in the Home Guard, which gave me plenty of openings for funny cracks.

I still have a photo of Zakky taken at the reception. My mother had asked him to be a groomsman, and he looked very dashing in hired morning-dress, holding his glass and laughing. He was willing to be happy for my mother, when he would never be happy for himself. And behind him in the photo is Rosemary Thomas, looking at him as if she wanted to eat him. Even now, when I look at it, it makes me shudder.

That Christmas Zakky got his chance. Major Newsam took him up for an interview at the War Office, and apparently he chattered French and English and German and Polish like a bird, and they grabbed him like he was the best thing since sliced bread.

He came back for a fortnight's leave in May 1944, in the uniform of the Intelligence Corps. He was truly happy, I think, for that fortnight. Southern England was, by that time, as packed with allied soldiers as an egg is full of meat, and he knew at last he was going to have his feast of death. He wasn't even eighteen, but he'd have passed for twenty-five with his hair cropped.

We went for a last walk before he left. My bottom field was full of Shermans under camouflage, and the Yank tank-crews bivouacked. He was quickly among them, shaking hands and laughing and talking about killing Nazis. It was pretty crazy and pretty painful, because the Yanks kept looking at each other and tapping their heads with their fingers, once he'd passed. I was bloody terrified he'd see them, because the little bulge at the back of his battle-dress collar told me the deadly knife was still there.

Walking home, we met Rosemary Thomas in the lane outside our house. I think she'd come looking for him. They went off together, his arm around her waist, natural as any young couple, laughing.

But I shuddered. He could afford to laugh, because he was going to kill. He could afford to love, because he was going to die. He was like a dragonfly that only lives a few days of summer; a dragonfly that is a gaudy killer.

I thought of him on D-Day. D-Day was a strange time for us Home Guard. Endless streams of allied planes flying east, where once there had been endless streams of Germans flying west. Endless streams of American armour pouring through our village, where once we'd stood expecting streams of German panzers.

In one day we became pointless. No one left to fight; no one even left to train. Our hands full of the very latest, useless guns. Newsam told me an order was coming out, to disband us, with thanks. We'd never fired a shot in anger; only blanks at friends.

Still, there was the harvest to get in. The hay was early that year. And that night I first met Shirley Harris, as we gathered round the radio in the pub to listen to the news from Normandy.

He never wrote.

There was one snippet about him in the local paper.

BIRSBY MAN WINS MILITARY MEDAL.

Major Newsam tried to find out more from his mates at the War Office. He got very little, except that Zakky had been promoted to sergeant. And a hint of cloak-and-dagger. Raids behind enemy lines, co-operation with the French Maquis, throats cut and no questions asked. A very dirty war indeed.

'Not my kind of war,' said Newsam. 'Not my kind of war at all.'

And then, nothing. VE day passed with great rejoicing, our village green packed with trestle tables, hung with red, white and blue bunting left over from the Coronation, the Silver Jubilee, Queen Victoria's birthday, for all I knew. We choked with the dust as we hung it up. A little band played for dancing, and women danced with women and children. Then VJ day, and the men began coming home, and still nothing. Six weeks later I married Shirley Harris. There was nothing to stop us. My mother had gone to live with the Major, in a country club he was trying to haul back to life further along the south coast.

And then, towards the back-end of 1945, I got home from a cattle auction, and Shirley met me in the yard and said,

'You've got a visitor.'

She looked scared to death, and she's not the nervous sort. So I went in feeling very proprietorial, and rather angry.

He was sitting at the kitchen table. Shirley had given him a cup of tea and a piece of home-made cake, as she did with everybody who called. He'd let the tea go cold, and rolled her good cake into tiny dark balls on the plate. Our kitchen was full of . . . the smell of him? The *vibes* of him? The only thing I can compare it to was the atmosphere at the funeral of a friend who had committed suicide. It was that black.

I made myself shake hands. His hand was very bony and cold. His hair was cropped like a convict's; you could see the white scalp showing through the black stubble. His flamboyant moustache was gone. So was any glint of life in his eyes; they were like two holes burnt in a grey blanket.

I said I was glad to see him, but I wasn't. I asked him whether he'd been demobbed. He said,

'They have stopped killing Nazis. Germany is full of Nazis but they are making them into burgomasters now. Because they are the only ones left who can run that country.' I noticed he was wearing one of those awful demob suits; it hung on him as it might have hung on a rail.

I tried to tell him about this and that; country gossip. But he cut me short, he didn't want to know.

I told myself he was still only a kid, not yet nineteen. But he wasn't. I even began to wish he had died, like the dragonfly, that gaudy killer. So that he didn't have to come back here and plague us. I began to worry he might ask after my mother . . .

In the end I said, straight out,

'What can I do for you, Zakky?'

'I wish to rent the mill. I will pay you fair rent.'

Should I have said no? So he might have drifted off and plagued somebody else? But all I wanted was him out of my kitchen, and the mill seemed a cheap price to pay. It still had its floors and roof, as the Home Guard had left it. I had no use for it.

We agreed a rent. I wasn't such a fool as to offer it to him for nothing, but I threw in some old furniture. Anything to get him out of my kitchen. He was death, walking.

They had glutted him with killing, then turned him loose on a world at peace.

And yet, it might still have worked for him. Lost in the world as he was, the mill became his fortress, the one place where his life had meaning. He kept it spotless, I was told. He even filled the little walled enclosure full of flowers. Only all the colours were those of the old Polish flag. A Polish flag now flew from the little flagpole we'd left on the roof. Inside, there was another Polish flag, draped round a photograph of the late General Sikorski. And there was a large radio, permanently tuned to Radio Warsaw.

But Poland was Communist now; full of Russians talking the language of pigs. We all knew he could never go home.

He scratched a living, mending machinery. Tom Hands offered him a partnership, but he refused. You never saw him talking to anybody round the village. But when he met any member of the old Home Guard, he would give a curt, abrupt nod of the head.

Only Rosemary Thomas did not despair. She beat against the walls of that mill, like a moth beating against a lamp. But, it seemed, in vain.

Yet she found fresh-killed rabbits on the pub doorstep some mornings. Killed by a knife-throw.

And then PC Morris from the next village came to see me. He'd heard rumours that Zakky had guns hung on the wall. Not shotguns, either. Guns from the war, people said . . .

I told him it was rubbish. They *must* be shotguns. I said I would be responsible for Zakky; see he didn't cause any trouble. Frankly, I told him anything I could think of, to get him to go away.

Zakky

To tell the truth, I feared for his life, if he tried to interfere.

And then, God help us, came the start of the post-war housing boom. Homes fit for heroes. Town vied with town. And our blessed district council decided to double the size of our village. On my land. By compulsory purchase order.

Mind you, they offered a fair price, and I had my eye on a bigger farm. I had no cause to grumble.

Till I heard the mill had to go, too.

I *pleaded* with the clerk to the council. I spent four hours trying to explain about Zakky. Didn't make a ha'p'orth of difference. Even ex-servicemen with valiant war-records must learn to make way for progress. Why, this whole scheme was *designed* for ex-servicemen. Mr Zakrewski might apply for one of the houses, if he was a married man with at least two children. But if he insisted on being awkward, that was surely a matter for the police . . .

Truly, I felt the ground open up beneath me.

I was still moving in that dark nightmare the following morning when I drove my tractor on to a too-steep bit of hillside, and it turned over on me. I was in a coma for six weeks, and my life was despaired of.

The morning Shirley finally drove me home from hospital, we came in on the road past Draggett's Mill.

It was gone; flat. All around, workmen were digging foundations for houses.

'Zakky . . .' I said. Full of dread, loss, a terrible feeling of letting people down.

'Gone,' said Shirley. 'Safe gone.'

'HOW?'

'Birsby Home Guard's last and best manoeuvre . . .'

'What *sort* of manoeuvre?'

'Old Comrades' Reunion. At Rosemary's pub. Zakky was formally requested to attend, or his old comrades would be *deeply* insulted. Given that Polish sense of honour, could Zakky refuse? Just for half an hour of course . . .'

'And then . . .?'

'Well, people began to drink toasts, with vodka bought off a Polish ship in Southampton. Oh, so *many* toasts. The late General Sikorski, and every member of his late government. Major Newsam had all their names off by heart, and nearly cracked his jaw pronouncing them. Zakky kept correcting him. Then Mr Churchill, President Roosevelt, President Truman, Chang Kai-shek, General de Gaulle, the R A F, the Home Guard, the Royal Navy. You name it, we had it. And Zakky couldn't refuse to drink to a single one, could he? On his Polish honour. And he was drinking neat vodka, and the rest were drinking vodka and water. Half the pub's glasses ended up smashed at the back of the pub fireplace. And every time a vodka glass was smashed, the flames would leap up nearly to the pub ceiling. A right little fire risk. Zakky loved every moment of it. Till he passed out cold.'

'Then?'

'Well, they had to carry him home to the mill, didn't they? And they took the rest of the vodka with them. And he'd left a fire burning at the mill. And . . . or so they said . . . they started drinking again, and smashing more glasses in the fireplace in true Polish fashion, and a full bottle of vodka somehow got broken in the fireplace, and . . . well, the whole mill went up in flames, and they only just got Zakky out in time. The mill was alight from top to bottom by the time the fire brigade got there. Weapons, bullets, hand-grenades, the lot went up. Quite a little fireworks display. There wasn't a lot left of the mill by the time they were finished. Even the stone walls fell in.'

'How did Zakky take it?'

'Well, they'd carried him back to the pub, overnight. And Rosemary was fluttering about him, tending to his hangover. And they all looked very sheepish, and told him what they'd done, and how sorry they were. And that they felt honour-bound to make amends for his loss.

And he could hardly blame them for going on in such a Polish way could he? Nor refuse their honourable desire to make amends. He went off with five hundred quid in his pocket. I think Major Newsam gave half . . .'

'What good is *money* to him?' I asked desperately.

'Oh, I wouldn't worry too much about him. Rosemary went with him.'

'Where, for God's sake?'

'Marbury, in Cheshire, according to Rosemary's letters. Hundreds of ex-Polish army up there. Starting to marry local girls, thinking of building their own church. She still has hopes he'll do the honourable thing, and marry her. Of course, she had a hand in the whole thing from the start . . .'

'*Women*,' I said.

'Women,' she agreed, smiling. 'What would you all do without us? Welcome home, Keith.'

The Making of Me

You see the state I'm in now, as I sit here.

Do not blame me. My grandfather made me what I am.

With one blow. In one minute.

I had a happy childhood, except for one thing. I hated being 'left with' people, when my parents went off somewhere. You could never tell what people would *do* with you, once your parents had gone.

Like my holy aunt, for instance. No sooner had my parents waved goodbye than one of her holy friends would turn up, hold my head between her hands, look deep into my eyes and ask if I said my prayers and hoped to go to heaven? I mean, what do you *say*?

Other times my aunt, who was Sally Army, would take me off round the streets, marching with the band. I quite liked the band, though I hated the way people stared at us. Especially when we stopped on some wet and windy corner and the Major began shouting wildly about Jesus Christ and Salvation, to the two men and a dog who'd stopped to listen.

He lisped. He kept asking people if they were 'thaved' or were still wallowing in their 'thins'. Some of my mates from school saw me standing next to him once, and I was regularly asked in the playground if I'd been 'thaved' from my 'thins'. For a whole three years, till I went to grammar school.

My unholy aunt wasn't so bad. She might condemn God non-stop, for letting little children die of diptheria or for sinking ships in storms, but at least she stayed home to do it, with nobody to hear but me. And she kept very good chocolate biscuits.

The person I really dreaded being left with, though, was my grandfather. He was not a *person*, like my mum and dad, or my little round laughing nana. He towered above me, six feet tall. I would sometimes glance up at him, as one might peer up in awe at a mountainous crag. The huge nose, the drooping moustache, the drooping mass of wrinkles. Then his eyes would peer down at me, too small, too close together, pale blue, wild and empty of everything but an everlasting, baffled rage. And my own eyes would scurry for cover, like a scared rabbit. He never spoke to me, and I never spoke to him, and thank God my parents never forced me to, as they would force me sometimes to kiss hairy-chinned old ladies.

There were old tales of his violence. How when his second child was born dead, he ripped the gas-cooker from the wall and threw it downstairs (and gas-cookers were solid cast-iron then, and weighed a ton). How when he came home drunk on a Saturday night, Nana and my eleven-year-old father would hear his step and run to hide in the outside wash-house, till he fell into a drunken sleep before the fire. And then Nana would stealthily rifle his pockets for the remains of his week's wages, and go straight and buy the week's shopping before he woke. And when he woke, he would think he'd lost all his money in his drunken stupor.

But the Great War had done for him. Unlike anybody else I knew, he had a Chest, because he'd been gassed in the trenches. His Chest made a fascinating symphony of noises at the best of times. So I would listen to it, rather than the chat round the meal-table. But when he was upstairs in bed, bad with his Chest, the whole house was silent and doom-laden, and my parents tiptoed about and talked in whispers.

He was also shell-shocked. Nana always had to be careful with the big black kettle she kept simmering on the hob to make a cup of tea. If it was allowed to boil, the lid would begin to rattle, making exactly the same noise as a distant machine-gun. And that would be enough to send him off into one of his 'dos', when he would imagine he was back in the hell of the trenches and would shout despairing orders, and I would be sent out for a walk till one of his powders settled him.

They said he had killed an Austrian soldier in a bayonet fight and taken his cap-badge. I was sometimes allowed to handle the strange square badge, to keep me quiet. It had a picture in brass of charging infantrymen, and strange, eastern, Hungarian writing. When Granda was *really* bad, he thought the dead Austrian had come back for his badge.

And, above all, he still drank. Perhaps to drown the memories he never spoke of. Oh, the silent agony of waiting to eat Sunday lunch, because of him, at our house; my mother fretting and the painful smell of good roast beef being singed to a crisp in the oven. Every ear cocked for his wavering footsteps. The strange bits of French songs or German marches that he would hum while he pushed his food unwanted round his plate.

Afterwards he would fall asleep with his mouth open. There was never any blackness for me like the blackness of the inside of his mouth.

But, while my parents were there, and the Nana I loved, he was just a fascinating monster, a fabulous beast. Safe to watch, like a tiger in a cage.

But being left alone with him . . .

A dreadful silence always fell. Perhaps he thought he had nothing in his mind fit for a child's ears. And my childish prattle, which so made the other grown-ups laugh, just got on his shell-shocked nerves.

Once, without warning, he clouted me across the ear. I think I wasn't so much hurt as *outraged*. Nobody had ever hit me, except my father twice, and that after plenty of warnings. The unfairness of it made the world reel about me. He told my father, afterwards, that I turned to him with tears in my eyes and said,

'Why did you hit me, grandfather?'

It sounds like something out of a Victorian novelette. But it must have cut him to his shell-shocked heart. When my parents returned they found me barricaded safely inside the outside loo, and him rocking with his head in his hands, full of agonized remorse that he had hit that innocent bairn. And vowing never to do it again till the day he died, or might his hand wither and drop off.

The innocent bairn wasn't slow to make the most of such an opening. Next time I was left with him, I found him still silent, but strangely obedient. I soon grasped he would do anything I wanted, just to keep me happy.

To be honest, I don't think I meant to be cruel: I wasn't a cruel child. But I had suffered a kind of personal earthquake at his hands, and I was very keen to prove his present mood would last, and the earthquake wouldn't happen again.

And I had a hopeless yearning to imitate my father, who was the engineer at the gasworks, and to me, a great wizard who dwelt among roaring furnaces and stamping carthorses, among great heaps of smoking slag and clouds of green gas, and who could start great steel dinosaurs of engines with one push of his small shoulder to an eight foot flywheel.

I wanted to make a *machine*. A machine of brass and steel that swung rhythmically and jangled loudly, and flashed with steel and brass.

I asked Granda to get Nana's washing-line.

He did.

I asked that he string it round the room from the hook on the kitchen door where her apron hung, to the rail above the kitchen range where she dried her tea-towels; from the handle of the cupboard to the hooks on the Welsh dresser. When it was firmly secured, we proceeded to hang from it every pot, pan, ladle and spoon in her well-stocked kitchen.

I pulled on the line. Everything swung, danced, jangled with the most satisfying cacophony. It was like entering into a new world.

Two hours later they found me still happily pulling and clanging, with my grandfather cowering in the depths of his chair with his hands pressed over his shell-shocked ears.

He had kept his word; he had not laid a hand on the innocent bairn. I don't know why he didn't strangle me; it must have been a close-run thing. Even I was scared at what I'd done – afterwards. When I saw the look on my father's face.

And then my unholy aunt fell ill, and was rushed to hospital and not expected to live. Suddenly the family were going to see her every night, and my mother thought that hospital was no place to take a child. From now on I was going to be left with my grandfather not once a month, but every night. A terrifying desert of silence and strangeness stretched before me. If I'd had any pity to spare from myself, I might have pitied Granda. But I was just plain terrified. What were we going to *say?* What were we going to *do* in that desert of time? I went, that first evening, thinking the end of the world, so often foretold by my holy aunt, was upon me.

I settled myself in the deepest chair, behind a mass of old comics I'd read ten times already. But the *Wizard* (and the famous Wilson, who had run the three-minute mile at the Berlin Olympics when he was a hundred and twenty years old, because he lived on rare herbs) had no charms that night.

I furtively eyed my strange sighing Beast as his Chest made its odd symphony of noises, and the terrifying sweet smell of sick old man came through the air to my cringing nostrils. I did not want to breathe the air he breathed. As my mother might have said about something I'd picked up in the street, I did not know where that air might have been. It might still have had bits in it from the trenches of the Great War, where dead men hung rotting on the barbed wire. Particles of poison gas; or the dying breath breathed out by the dead Austrian . . .

85

In the soft glow of the gas-mantle, his face was all wrinkled and shadowed pits, mysterious as craters of the moon. He was fiddling with the tap of the gas-light, fixing a little bit of wire round it. Perhaps it was his way of keeping me at bay, as my comics were my way of keeping him at bay.

He had dragged out of some cupboard a large old stained tea-chest. It was full of strange shapes, trapped in tangled coils of wire. The strange shapes drew me irresistibly; perhaps I had some wild hope of building another jangle-machine. I put a tentative hand inside. There was the most huge rusty hammer I'd ever seen . . . a long weird knife in a scabbard. I tugged at the knife; it resisted. I tugged harder . . . then harder. It leapt out of my hand, dragging behind it, in a web of tangled wire, a queerly shaped, huge brass tap, and a short brass cylinder. They all fell on the floor with a terrible bang. He swung round, ever-jumpy . . .

I gabbled out, before he could hit me,

'What's that funny tap, Granda?'

He picked up the tap, as if he hadn't seen it in a long time.

'By,' he said dreamily, 'that's a spare tap left over from the old *Mauretania*. Finest and fastest ship in the world, she was. Held the Blue Riband of the Atlantic for twenty years. The day she was launched – she had no funnels or nothing, mind – the shipyard workers got up steam in a little donkey-boiler in the bows. The old Morrie was the only liner ever launched wi' steam up. And when she sailed on her maiden voyage, people lined the banks of the Tyne for eight miles to bid her Godspeed. As if the King was passin' . . . and when she came home from her last voyage, to be broken up to make razor blades, the people lined up again to say goodbye to her. Look, here's the pictures.' And there, on the wall, were two photographs of the old Morrie sailing and the old Morrie coming home. And she looked the same in both.

'Why did they break her up? She looks as good as new.'

'Aye, but she was tired *inside*,' he said. 'Things look the same, but they get tired inside.' There was something in his voice I couldn't face. So I held up the short brass cylinder before the silence came back like the frozen Arctic.

'That's the lens of the film-projector that showed the first movie ever shown in North Shields. The show was held in the Temperance Hall, and it cost a penny to get in. Fatty Arbuckle was the star – he got sent to prison in the end. We saw Charlie Chaplin through that. Rudolph Valentino. No talkies of course – just a lady playing the piano for the exciting bits.'

'How did you get it?'

'George Costigan gave it to me in Guthrie's Bar, the night the old King died . . .'

'And what's this?' I held up a worn long block of rubber.

'That's the brake-block off me old bike – the one I used to ride round Holywell Dene, when I was courting your nana. I was taking that brake-block off, the night your dad was born . . .' A new kind of awe swept over me. My mother had often talked about the night *I* was born (and what a hard time I'd given her, and how she'd almost died of me), and that was mysterious enough. But the night my *dad* was born . . . that was as incredibly far off as the Pharaohs building the pyramids.

We were off in style now. Every object told a story. The dead rose up and walked again. Admiral Jellicoe and Earl Kitchener of Khartoum. Kaiser Bill and Marie Lloyd. Lloyd

George and Jack the Ripper. They streamed out of my grandfather as they might have streamed out of the first cinema-projector to show a film in North Shields.

Only once was he silent. About the long knife in the scabbard. He took it in his hand and was silent, then he put it back in the box. I knew it was the bayonet that had killed the Austrian, for his face went grey, and his eyes were far away. I knew he hated it. I also knew he would never throw it away. Just like the cap-badge.

'What did you do in the trenches – in between?' I asked.

'I'll tell yer.' He pulled out a steel helmet, thick with rust. 'See that little hole in the top?'

'Is it a bullet-hole?'

He actually laughed. 'No, no. It's a screw-hole. We used to pull the screw out and stick a nail through the hole, and stick a candle on the nail. So we could see to play cards. Look – you can still see a bit o' candle-grease. I was good at cards – three-card brag, a quick game – it didn't matter if you were interrupted, like. I won a lot o' money. Lot o' fellers still owe me money, but they're dead. So I took a little thing from their kit, instead. To remember them by. See . . .' He reached up and took down his shaving-tackle from above the sink.

'That's Gerry Henry's shaving brush, and Mannie Webber's bowl, and Tommy Malbon's mirror . . . Good chums, every one.'

Now we were both silent, and it was all right. For I knew who was in the silence now. The good chums, every one.

It was Granda who broke the silence. 'There was a joke as we used to have, us Shields lads out there: